The Sultan's Organ

Jonathan Gathorne-Hardy was born in Edinburgh in 1933. He was educated at Bryanston and from there gained a scholarship to Trinity College, Cambridge, where he read history. He then worked for fifteen years in advertising and publishing. He has written over twenty books, including an autobiography *Half an Arch*, (winner of the JR Ackerley prize), *Kinsey: Sex The Measure Of All Things* which was adapted into a successful film starring Liam Neeson, *The Rise and Fall of the British Nanny*, *A Life of Gerald Brenan*, which was used in the making of the film of *South from Granada* and *The Public School Phenomenon 1587-1977*. He lives in North Norfolk with his wife, the painter and writer Nicky Loutit.

*The publisher is indebted to Dolf Mootham,
Eimear McBride, Ray Rumsby and Oliver Frankl
for their generous help and support.*

UNESCO *City of Literature* ™

First published in 2017

by Propolis Books
The Book Hive,
53 London Street,
Norwich, NR2 1HL

cover design & art **studio medlikova**

A CIP record for this book
is available from the British Library

Printed and bound by TJ International, Padstow, Cornwall,

Jonathan Gathorne-Hardy

The Sultan's Organ

The Epic Voyage of Thomas Dallam and his extraordinary
Musical Instrument to Constantinople in 1599
and his Time in the Palace and Harem
of the Ottoman Sultan

propolis

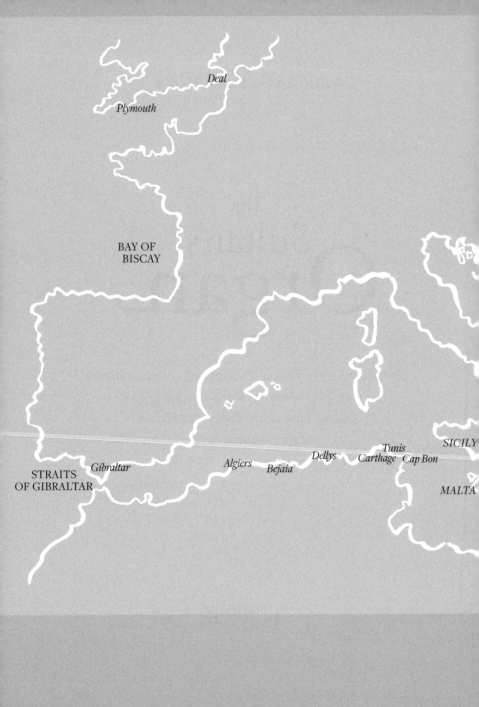

Deal

Plymouth

BAY OF
BISCAY

STRAITS
OF GIBRALTAR

Gibraltar

Algiers

Bejaia

Dellys

Tunis
Carthage Cap Bon

SICILY

MALTA

THE BLACK SEA

THE
BOSPHORUS

Constantinople

Tenedos

Lamia
Patra   Volos   Chios
Cyllene
Zante   Cape Gata

                    Samos
                        Rhodes   Scanderoon
Cerigo   Carpathos   Aleppo
                        Cassos
        Crete   Famagusta
                            Paphos CYPRUS

THE
MEDITERRANEAN

In memory of Dolf Mootham,
the most generous of friends

CHAPTER 1

A Gathering Crisis

The Strangling of the Brothers

Early in 1595 the Ottoman Sultan Murad III died in Constantinople's Topkapi Palace – partly, as a result of incessant over-indulgence in the concubines of his harem.

[1]Eleven days later the new Sultan, Mehmed III, arrived in Constantinople. It was the coldest winter for fifty years, snow sweeping down from Russia, blown by furious winds. Nevertheless, his accession immediately set off an event so cruel and ruthless that it appals us even today. Mehmed's nineteen younger brothers, many very young, were led out of the harem, circumcised if they had not been already and were then strangled with a silk handkerchief (or possibly with a bowstring – the point was to prevent the spilling of sacred Ottoman blood). The strangling was done with great dexterity by mutes, who were kept in the palace for such tasks and were experts in their duties. One brother was only eleven and in the middle of eating some roast chestnuts when he was called out. 'Let me eat my chestnuts first,' he said, 'and strangle me afterwards.' The graves of the little princes are in one of the garden mausoleums of the Hagia Sophia (*Ayasofya*) mosque.

Mehmed III, aged twenty-nine, was not a pleasant character.[2] Lazarro Soranzo's *Ottomano,* written in 1598 and translated in 1603, describes a weak and sadistic sensualist who enjoyed killing and torturing people, particularly women. When younger, Mehmed was said to have had 'the breasts of women torn off with red hot tongs', and it was also said that he had murdered his grandmother 'with his own hands'. Another time, hearing that a scholar in Konya (a large town in south-central Turkey) had spoken disparagingly of him, he had, on the spot, ordered that 2,000 students there be put to death. But this vicious man must have known some of his younger brothers intimately. [3]They were strangled in front of him, as was the custom, and he is reported to have torn at his beard in grief and horror.

This terrible event, although expected, caused almost equal horror in the court itself – particularly, of course, among the mothers of the young boys. Its reverberations went round Europe and struck with special force in London, most keenly among a group of wealthy men closely involved with Constantinople. These were the merchants of the Levant Company.

Ottoman Realpolitik

The merchants' concerns over the murder of the nineteen young princes were not due to fastidiousness or even remotely humanitarian, and it should be noted that, as so often with such events in the Ottoman Empire at that time, these acts were not unique to Turkey, nor were they especially unusual.

[4]Numerous French princes, for example, were murdered in these early centuries, as were the relatives of the Mughal emperors in Delhi. In England, popular distaste at this Ottoman practice was expressed, among other ways, in the plays of Shakespeare. In *Henry IV, Part 2,* for instance, Henry V chides his brothers on their fear at his accession – 'This is the English not the Turkish court.'

But, in fact, in this respect it could be argued that English practice was worse than the Ottomans.[5] In 2006 an interesting paper in the journal *History of the Family* that pointed out how, in what is known as the Cousins' Wars, murder as an instrument in gaining and protecting the crown was very common. Between 1377 and 1558, when Elizabeth came to the throne, forty-seven members of the royal family were murdered by their relatives.

What interested the authors of the paper was that *cousins* were eliminated, not direct lineal descendants; they argued that since direct descendants have fifty per cent monarchic genes it was, even if unconsciously, the reason they should be protected. The theory, while of course another example of murder to gain or keep the crown, is to some extent contradicted, or at least not supported, by the Ottoman practice, where it was exactly those extra monarchic genes which were removed.

All told, about eighty Ottoman princes were murdered. This may seem a lot compared to forty-seven but, in fact, the Wars of Succession between the houses of Lancaster and York, (The War of The Roses, which form the subject of most of Shakespeare's historical plays), the struggles of the Tudors and the religious civil wars in sixteenth-century France were all due, or largely due, to a lack of dynastic clarity. Not tens, but hundreds of thousands perished in these wars.

It was this situation which terrified the Ottomans. And they were even more prone to it than the countries of the West. Similar civil wars had plagued the dynasty early in the fifteenth century. There was no strict law of succession until 1607. The older princes were usually dispersed and the throne went to the one who reached Constantinople and the imperial treasury first. When Selim II died in 1574 after falling off his horse, probably drunk, his mother Norbanu concealed his death completely and hid his corpse in an icebox until her favourite son Murad III could get to the capital from Manisa in Anatolia, after which Selim's body – and death – was revealed.

This practice of institutional murder grew steadily after Mehmed II's conquest of Constantinople in 1453, from which it is convenient to date the rise of the Ottoman dynasty onto the international scene. In fact the practice can be traced back, as it is in Caroline Finkel's magnificent work, to the thirteen hundreds. Mehmed II himself executed two brothers. Selim I (Sultan 1512–20) killed three sons, three brothers and four nephews. This system, like that of concubines, to which we'll come when we explore the Sultan's harem, grew up precisely to prevent the situation in Europe. They

3

were typical examples of Ottoman *realpolitik* and they succeeded. England might have done better to have copied both.

But if it was not due to their humanity, why did the merchants of the Levant Company become so agitated by what took place in the Topkapi Palace in 1595? To understand this, and much of the story about to unfold, it is necessary to know something of Levant Company history.

The Levant Company

[6]Until the eighteenth century, root crops were not available for farmers to feed their cattle and sheep during the winter and supplies of hay were insufficient to last. Enough animals had to be kept for breeding, but each year a great slaughter took place at the end of autumn. The meat was then salted down into barrels. But salt was also in short supply, so preservation was patchy. It is a mistake however to believe that spices became popular to disguise the taste of rotting meat; they were expensive and eating decaying flesh can be very dangerous. But they were in demand, apart from anything to elevate the taste of a predominantly bland cuisine – as they are today.

This was true all over Europe. It was compounded by another consideration, however, which was that the other main preservative was sugar. This meant that teeth – while you still had them – became pitted with holes, leading to decay and often very bad breath. Spices could disguise this as well. (Toothpicks became essential. [7]At the court of Lucrezia Borgia they were scented.)

The Levant in the sixteenth century comprised the whole sweep of the eastern Mediterranean (Levant from the French *lever* – to rise, since the sun rises in the east). It also included a considerable stretch of the North African coast and many of the large islands in the Aegean. And the principal trading centres for spices were Venice and, in particular, Constantinople.

The vicissitudes of this trade during the first seventy years of the century are complicated, but can be skimmed. Spices in fact originated in the Far East coming to Constantinople (and Venice) either through Russia and Persia

(Iran) or up from the Red Sea, through Syria via Aleppo and Alexandria. But the Levant was also a source of wine, olive oil, silk, cotton and currants – particularly popular in Elizabethan England. About 2,000 tons were imported annually. England could in return supply cloth, woollens, tin, pewter, lead and rabbit skins.

The nascent trade directly with Ottoman Turkey stopped in 1535. Partly this was because it was very expensive. The overland routes required the payment of many middlemen along their long, slow, winding way. But mainly it was because of pirates.

In the sixteenth century, pirates dominated the seas from the Levant up around Europe and even into the North Sea. In the Mediterranean, where they were especially concentrated, their activities were compounded by the hostility of the Ottoman navy (of which, in fact, most of the pirates were an unofficial, uncontrollable arm). It quite simply became too dangerous for England to continue trading in the Levant.

However, it was much less dangerous for France. France had treaties with the Ottomans as early as 1535 and paid tolls and duty on her trade; one of the main French ports, Marseilles, was relatively close to Constantinople. The same was true of Venice – an aggressive imperial power with territories all down the Adriatic and among the larger Greek islands. (The Republic, defeated by France in 1509, was in fact declining. But the decline of great nations is never noticed at first, either by them or their rivals.)

The spice trade now came up through Europe, via Venice and France, and from Portugal trading directly with the Far East. Rich Dutch traders bought from all three sources and sold from Antwerp. It was much easier and safer for England to pay high Dutch prices (which could be passed on) than risk the Levant.

But during the 1560s and '70s there were a number of significant developments. First, there was a huge increase in firepower for European and English ships. Second, the Ottoman Empire – at that time the most powerful in Europe – had been thought to have a navy invincible in the

Mediterranean. But in 1571, the Ottoman galleys were defeated at the battle of Lepanto (largely by the Spanish, and as a result of the new firepower. Cervantes fought in this battle and permanently damaged his right hand). The Ottomans were not invincible. A journey to the Levant had become slightly less dangerous.

But the intense and growing rivalry between England and Spain, culminating in war, was the clincher. Spain conquered Portugal, and in the late 1560s the Netherlands after long subjection, revolted against Spain. Antwerp, in the thick of these struggles and ultimately to remain under Spanish control for several decades, ceased, as far as England was concerned to be a viable route for spices and other Levantine imports. However it had long been clear that immense profits could be made in the spice trade. Two leading London merchants decided to investigate the possibility of re-opening a route.

[8]The first of these, Edward Osborne, was an interesting man – and a courageous one. Born in 1530, he was apprenticed to Sir William Hewitt of the Clothworkers' Guild. When he was fifteen, a nursemaid dropped Hewitt's baby daughter Anne from an apartment on London Bridge into the torrent below. Osborne at once leapt in after her. This was a brave act, since the Thames was a very different river then. Osborne rescued the baby and – like a fairy story – eventually married her. He was left Hewitt's business, his London mansion, the London Bridge apartment, and most of his Yorkshire estates. By 1571 he owned a ship and was trading with Scandinavia and also Spain and Portugal, though this was now increasingly difficult to do. In 1593 he became Lord Mayor.

[9]Osborne was joined by a younger man, Richard Staper, to whom he was connected by both business and marriage. Much less is known about Staper, except that he was eventually knighted. His epitaph in St Helen's, Bishopsgate reads: 'The greatest merchant of his time.' He traded with Brazil and, like Osborne, with Spain and Scandinavia. These men could raise money.

In 1578, after three years of manoeuvring and bribing, they were able to send a factor of Osborne's, William Harborne, to Constantinople to manoeuvre and bribe on their, and the Queen's, behalf. He went overland for safety and under the official protection of the French.

Harborne was a formidable figure. He could, if necessary, lose his temper – he once struck the Turkish Lord High Admiral for saying the crews of English ships were no better than pirates (often true). More importantly, and very unusually, he spoke fluent Turkish and often dressed in Turkish clothes. He argued persuasively that the English and the Ottomans had a common enemy in Spain, an argument of some force after Lepanto, and that it would benefit both if English traders had the same trading privileges (capitulations) as the French and Venetians. Above all, he had considerable personal charm.

The Sultan and his entourage were duly charmed. Flowery exchanges began to flow between the two monarchs. Murad III addressed the queen as a 'cloud of the most pleasant raine and fountain of nobleness and vertue.' The cloud of raine answered in kind, to the 'most sovereign monarch of the east' to whom 'she wished many happy and fortunate yeares.' Eventually, by a treaty signed in June 1580, Murad granted the English the capitulations they had asked for. Elizabeth granted similar privileges to Turkish merchants in England. She also pointed out tactfully that a lot of Englishmen, captured by pirates, were held as slaves in the Sultan's dominions. This treaty required that these should be set free. (It was soon evident that the petty kings and pashas, nominally subject to the Sultan, usually ignored him here.)

Harborne returned to London. The French ambassador in Constantinople, Monsieur de Germigny, who, along with the *bailo* (representative) of Venice, had watched with growing fury as this Englishman, ostensibly under French protection, had been scheming and working to share in France's valuable trading privileges, at once distributed massive bribes and had all the English capitulations cancelled.

Harborne hurried back to Constantinople but failed to have the capitulations renewed. Nevertheless, he made it clear to Osborne and Staper that this was almost certainly temporary. They therefore went ahead raising money, choosing colleagues and, above all, negotiating with the Queen and her most important ministers, notably Francis Walsingham and William Cecil, for a Royal Charter. Cecil had become Lord Burghley in 1571 (but by the time our narrative proper begins in 1599 he had died and been followed as one of Elizabeth's chief advisers by his son, Robert Cecil.) A charter was essential because only a chartered company could enforce the monopoly essential in a risky business and extract duty from its members. Furthermore a Royal Charter was necessary if Harborne was to be an accredited ambassador. This alone would ensure he would have the ear of the Sultan and the respect of his leading ministers. The Queen was perfectly happy with this – but the merchants must pay for everything. The costs would be enormous – indeed had already been enormous. The merchants thought the Queen, who would certainly benefit considerably, should share them. The Queen thought the opposite.

Elizabeth won. When Harborne, now chief representative of what was in effect, if not name, the Turkey Company, finally sailed, carried by the *Great Susan* on 14 January 1583, he was commissioned as 'Ambassador'. (All ships sailing to the Levant tried to do so in winter, when pirates were less active.) He arrived in Constantinople on 29 March, an incredibly quick voyage. It often took six months, sometimes longer.

At once Monsieur de Germigny and the Venetian *bailo*, Signor Mansini, began to manoeuvre feverishly. As well as more bribes, the French ambassador said it would be the end of the Franco–Turkish alliance if Harborne was 'received' – the crucial event when he was presented to the Sultan. [10]Signor Marsini was authorised to spend 15,000 zecchini in bribes, (at a very rough estimate, about £120,000 today), but it was money spent in vain.

On 24 April 1583, Harborne kissed the hem of the Sultan's garment and gave him the most important present of all the many presents and bribes he had so far distributed and would distribute: the present from Queen Elizabeth, paid for, like all the others, by the Levant merchants. This consisted, as was usual, of £500 worth of cloth and silver-gilt plate (silver thinly coated in gold) and, less usual, an assortment of dogs – mastiffs, spaniels, bloodhounds and 'two little dogges in coats of silk'. But it was the main item which astonished, delighted and deeply impressed the Turks. This was a clock, but a clock with endless and ingenious mechanical adjuncts – 'a forest with trees of silver, among which were deere chased with dogges and men on horseback following, men drawing of water, others carrying mine oare on barrows. [England at that time was the largest producer of tin in Europe and it was one of her main exports to Turkey.] On toppe of the clocke stood a castle and on the castle a mill.' All these were of silver and worked like – probably by – clockwork. 'The clocke was round inset with jewells.'

The extraordinary effect this mechanical clock-toy had on the Ottomans sank deep. It seemed to justify at a stroke the terrifying amount the merchants had paid out. For this item alone £1,082.6s.7d (more than around £100,000 today).

And one should note here certain *leitmotifs* that will reappear. The entire mechanism of the Ottoman government, especially as regards the furiously competing foreigners, revolved around 'presents' and bribes. The present to the Sultan from the corresponding monarch (or the Doge in Venice) was the most important. All officials expected to be bribed, and obviously the officials and ministers who had the Sultan's ear were the most likely to be so: the grand vizier, the mufti (religious leader), the lord treasurer, the bostancıbaşı (head gardener, commander of the Sultan's guards, captain of the Royal Barge, chief executioner), the çokador ağa (head valet), the lord high admiral, the hoja (old tutor of the Sultan), the aga of the Janissaries, the chief eunuchs, (both black and white) and often other figures too. The queen mother, or valide, was also very important. Some at least of these had to be kept on side – and since the Ottomans accepted bribes and presents from anyone and everyone, the expenses became enormous. By the end of the Turkish Company's charter the merchants said they had paid out £40,000 (around half a million today. For this sort of estimate I usually follow Sarah Bradford and her fine book on Lucrezia Borgia.).

The expenses were enormous, but so too were the profits. Harborne rapidly set up consuls and trading centres in Egypt, Syria (Aleppo) and Palestine, and soon in Algiers, Tunis and some of the Greek (then often Venetian) islands – in Zante, Chios and Crete. Apart from the obvious convenience of warehouses to store goods, company officers *in situ* and so on, these trading centres meant negotiations were not subjected to the urgency of arriving or departing of ships, and proper bargains could be struck. Between 1583 and 1588, nineteen ships were chartered and twenty-two voyages made. Goods could sell in England for three or four times what they cost in the Levant. One cargo alone sold in England for £70,000 in 1588 (in Sarah Bradford's terms, nearly a million today).

And this trade now included something relatively new. The defeat at Lepanto and the wars with Venice and Persia meant that the Ottomans required military raw materials. The Pope had forbidden Europe to supply this sort of material but Protestant England could ignore this. [11]Harborne and subsequent traders brought wool especially for uniforms, steel as well as tin, and various metals from church property to be melted into ordinance.

A third *leitmotif* that was to be in play for some twenty years was England's war with Spain. We can see how badly Elizabeth felt she needed the Sultan – and of course she was right – from the Fugger Newsletters of the time. [12]Philip Edward Fugger was the head of a great banking house. His agents sent him regular reports from all the capitals of Europe. On 20 September 1586, for example, the agent in Madrid wrote that 'there is indeed a great rumour that his majesty intends next year to equip a great Armada and make an expedition against England.' All Europe was clearly buzzing with this. The agent then added another rumour: the Sultan, at Elizabeth's suggestion, planned to send 100 galleys against Spain. The Fugger agent in Constantinople confirmed this on 1 October 1586. 'The English Ambassador ... was recently with the Grand Vizier and urgently requested the equipment of a fleet against the King [of Spain].' The Sultan assured him that he 'would not be backward next spring, but that she must spare no effort on her part too.' The Ottomans, who had been defeated by Spain at Lepanto in the Adriatic, certainly wanted any ally they could get against her now, but at this point Murad III could not see why Spain should be quite so bothered by the English. Looking on the moderately accurate maps at the tiny dot thousands of miles away, he asked why Spain didn't just 'shovel them into the sea?'

It was against this background that a Spanish mission arrived in Constantinople determined to secure a treaty with the Sultan to neutralise any political alliance against them and so protect their flank and also to get a share of the huge Levantine trade profits. Everyone expected them to succeed – and at first they did. But Harborne at once mobilised large sums of money and lavish presents. The Fugger correspondent, watching fascinated, reported that 'contrary to all expectations, the Spanish mission has got the worst of it; the English embassy, with 5000 ducats which it has thrust into the maw of the Hoja [the old tutor] of the Sultan holds the field.' All the concessions to Spain were torn up. The mission was told that if the King of Spain 'desired to seek and obtain the friendship of the Sultan, he should send, like other Christian sovereigns, a regular and respectable embassy to the Porte.' Spain had failed.

After seven years, the Royal Charter of what had in effect been the Turkey Company expired. It took three years haggling and arguing to renew it. The haggling was, apart from the usual useless attempts to get the queen to share some of the expenses, partly because the merchants who had hitherto traded from Venice, but had recently been banned there, insisted they should be included. Finally, in 1592, a new company was incorporated with fifty-three merchants, of whom Osborne was the governor. In fact, he died soon after it was set up and Staper took over. The new body was called the Levant Company.

Crisis for the Levant Company

[13]Harborne had left Constantinople in August 1588, with thirty members of his suite and at huge expense. He coasted gloriously back on waves of

astonished admiration at England's amazing defeat of the Spanish Armada. The astonishment is hardly surprising; a superpower had been defeated by a tiny island, rather as if, a few years ago, Cuba had suddenly mobilised and destroyed the might of the American navy. [14]The amazing news had reached Indonesia within eighteen months.

He had appointed his secretary as his successor. Edward Barton was only twenty-six, but he had been with Harborne for seven or eight years and knew exactly what the position entailed. And he had been tested. In 1583, one of the first ships chartered by the Turkish Company, the *Jesus,* had been seized by pirates in the port of Tripoli. It seems the company's French factor had been secretly cheating. He and the innocent captain were hanged on the spot, and the twenty-six English crew and passengers were 'cast into prison, of whom through famine, thirst and stinke of prison, eleven died and the rest like to die.' The Queen complained, Murad agreed something should be done, and Harborne sent his young secretary out to see that it was. He was successful. He was then twenty-one.

[15]By twenty-six he was, according to a contemporary, Fynes Moryson, courteous, affable, good looking and cheerful, which the Turks particularly liked 'for they love not a sad countenance, and much regard a comely person'. They also appreciated that he, like Harborne, could speak fluent Turkish and often dressed in Turkish clothes, to the degree that when he died the Turks said, mistakenly, he had become a Muslim. (All the rest of the foreign community used interpreters. The diplomatic language in Constantinople was Italian.)

There were critical comments from John Sanderson, one of the chief figures in both the Turkey and the Levant companies. [16]Sanderson said Barton kept a dissolute house, was fat, drank too much and was a womaniser, which he demonstrated by saying he had taken the attractive young wife of the exiled King of Fez as his mistress. No doubt she was not the king's only wife and, if true, none of his other criticisms would have particularly bothered the Turks – on the contrary. And all Sanderson's comments about almost everyone were waspish. He was a prig, bad-tempered and rude. He had also quarrelled with Barton. (They all seemed to have had rows with each other, both within the embassies and, not surprisingly, between them. The diplomatic circle in Constantinople was minute and except for Barton and Harborne, they did not mix with the Ottomans. Proximity and stress in a very foreign country led to paranoia and fierce quarrels.)

Barton's six years running the company in Constantinople were bedevilled by lack of money and by the reluctance of the Levant merchants to disgorge the large sums necessary for presents. He was supposed to collect four per cent of the value of all goods the ships and the company dealt with (consulage). Each ship, and each owner and his factor, although under the protection of the company, traded separately, and it had always been difficult to collect what they owed. With no charter – i.e. no company – it was almost impossible. In 1590 Barton wrote to Burghley saying that only one 'small ship' of a Mr Hamden had paid anything at all. He also had to engage in endless diplomatic moves and counter-moves – successful up to the point where, by dint of forging a letter proving that Jacques de Savary de Lancosme, who had replaced the French ambassador Monsieur de Germigny, was in the pay of Spain. As a result Lancosme was expelled and Barton helped get Sieur de Brèves appointed. But he also had the endless task of wooing important Ottoman officials. Since not yet accredited 'Ambassador' he could not approach the Sultan, but the mufti was still friendly, as was the hoja, the ex-tutor. The grand vizier, Sinan Pasha, also seemed well disposed to the plump and charming Barton. (So broke was Barton at one time, and so friendly the mufti, that Barton was able to borrow £1,500 from him. The mufti's growing irritation when he wasn't paid back went on rumbling for years.)

But very soon there were anxieties about the non-appearance of a present from the new company. [17]In January 1593, the Fugger agent reported Barton as saying that the ship carrying the present had been captured by the Spanish near Gibraltar. 'This appears somewhat doubtful to people here,' wrote the agent, 'for the Englishman has used this excuse before.' In April, Barton said a new present had now been dispatched, which was true – except it didn't arrive for five months.

Then in August 1593 there occurred a crisis in which Barton once again showed the courage and resource which had helped him solve the seizure of the *Jesus*. It also showed his knowledge of the oriental mind. The grand vizier, Sinan Pasha, was in Hungary where Turkey was fighting the Holy Roman Emperor. His stand-in, Ferhad Pasha, was a hard, ruthless man with a violent temper who hated the English.

A number of political prisoners had escaped from the Tower of the Black Sea. The governor was summarily executed, but the barber–surgeon at the English embassy, John Field, was also arrested on Ferhad Pasha's orders and threatened with death. He had carried a letter to one of the prisoners. Barton went to the acting grand vizier and tried to get Field released. Ferhad Pasha lost his temper and said he would arrest Barton as well.

There existed a procedure whereby Turkish subjects could petition the Sultan, but it required courage to use it. A frivolous petition could lead to execution. Barton now followed the procedure. He had himself rowed in a small boat to just offshore from a little mosque where Murad went to pray. When the Sultan appeared, Barton stood up, holding the scroll of his petition to his head, as was the custom. After a while, a dwarf (the court was full of dwarves) who had helped Barton before (and been rewarded) beckoned him to the shore and took the petition to the Sultan.

In fact it was not so much a petition as a threat. Unless the grand vizier made instant and honourable amends for the insult to Her Majesty Queen Elizabeth in the person of her ambassador (which he technically was not at that moment) Barton would not deliver her present. He would also have to see if his great queen would allow this insult to go unpunished.

The Sultan replied at once. If Barton went within the hour to the grand vizier's court, Ferhad Pasha would give him a gown of cloth-of-gold, which the Sultan had that moment dispatched for him. Everyone was amazed, '... especially,' wrote Richard Wragg, about to arrive on the *Ascension* with the present, 'the French and Venetian ambassadors, who never in the like case ... [would] durst have attempted so bold an enterprise.'

And one might note two other things about this incident. The culture of presents worked so well because the recipients *wanted* their presents. Quite often, the Sultan and his ministers seemed to play off the French or Venetians, say, against the English, just to get more of them. And it was reciprocal. The Ottomans gave as well as received. [18]Cloth-of-gold garments could be very valuable. Gold thread consisted of a strip of gold flattened by hammers and then made even thinner by being dragged through dye holes and 'wrapped or laid over a thread of silk by twisting it with a wheel'. Gold and silver thread could be plaited together. We see a feeble echo of this in the braiding on the sleeves of naval officers and airline pilots today. [19]But its use could be so lavish in the sixteenth-century Ottoman court that the coffers of this empire – the richest in Europe – sometimes temporarily ran short because so much gold had gone into clothes and other decoration.

Then at last in October 1593, twenty months late, the present finally arrived. [20]Just before it was ceremoniously handed over, the *Ascension*, 'a new shippe,' wrote Wragg, 'very well appointed,' of 260 tons and a massive armament of twenty-seven guns, was sailed round and anchored just before the mosque where Barton had recently presented his 'petition'. Here she fired her salute of two volleys of small arms fire, two shots each, and the entire battery of cannon – billowing smoke, crashing explosions, more smoke. The Sultan loved this firework display and asked for it to be repeated for his Sultana, which it was two days later. It *was* a firework display, but one with an edge. It made clear why Spain couldn't just shovel England into the sea. The little dot was a powerful ally.

Finally, the presentation. This, also described by Wragg, was immensely elaborate, immensely long and immensely impressive. Barton arrived magnificently equipped in cloth-of-gold and cloth-of-silver. Seven gentlemen of his staff were in suits of satin, thirty further members in dark

French-russet livery. As he stepped ashore from the ferry, the *Ascension*, anchored nearby, once again exploded. Fifty heralds greeted him and accompanied him, on horseback, through the great courtyards of the palace. The significance is that, at this point, he *was* Queen Elizabeth. He passed row after row of bowing courtiers, pausing briefly to chat to Ferhad Pasha as if with an old friend. There followed a banquet of a hundred dishes. Finally, after further ceremonies, Barton stood in the present room. A pasha (high-ranking official) stepped each side of him, twisted their hands into the long cloth-of-gold sleeves of yet another gown just given to him from the Sultan, and marched him to Murad's throne. He bent and kissed the jewel-covered hand resting idly on the arm of the throne. He was then dragged backwards to the door where he was allowed to ask a brief question – might the English capitulations be renewed? The Sultan answered curtly 'Yes'. But he also, as a sign of favour, gave orders that the daily allowance of meat, hay, firewood and money given to the embassy be doubled. (An interesting item, this – some basic pay and provisions came from the Ottomans.)

Three thousand horsemen, said Wragg, accompanied Barton and his entourage to the landing stage and, as they embarked on the ferry, the *Ascension* set off a further series of deafening explosions.

But this respite was only temporary. Just over twelve months later, on 7 January 1595, Murad III died. For Barton, this was a serious blow: years of cultivating the Sultan and his officials and servants gone at a stroke. Not only the Grand Turk gone, but pashas changed, eunuchs, dwarves, mutes and the women of the harem now suddenly without influence and all swept away into the old seraglio (the old harem). He would have to re-weave his whole intricate network of support, re-bribe, give more presents, and now once again just as an agent, no longer an ambassador.

A blow to Barton, but to the Levant merchants something close to a catastrophe. They were immediately faced with the necessity of a new present to a new Sultan – Mehmed III.[21]

Where is the Queen's Present?

[22]The present only just given had cost about £2,070 (Harborne's estimate before he left). Wragg describes it as '12 goodly pieces of gilt plate, 36 garments of satin, 6 pieces of fine Holland and certain other things of good value'. There is a manuscript in the British Museum detailing a long list of expensive gifts at this time.

Barton realised immediately that the Levant merchants would be extremely reluctant to send another present so soon. Voyages to and from England, as we've seen, often took six months or longer. And the concept of time, partly as a result of the slowness of communication and travel, was more relaxed and more elastic than ours today. But by 20 September 1595, nine months after Murad's death, Barton had written to Robert Cecil who, as we saw, had followed his father as one of Elizabeth's chief ministers, to say that a present should be dispatched at once. The longer it is delayed 'the lesse affection it will represent'.[23] Quickest and most effective, Barton said, would be if the queen sent the present herself – why not 'a clocke in the form of a cocke' which he heard 'her Highness hath in one of her palaces?' It is clear from this that the memory of the extraordinary effect the company's clock had had before was still vivid in the merchant's mind.

The queen was not pleased by this suggestion – yet it was not totally unreasonable. [24]She personally had earlier invested £40,000 in the whole Levant project (her share of Drake's 'privateering' – i.e. piracy – against the Spaniards), so she was sharing in their profits, not to mention her revenues from the customs dues the company paid. Why shouldn't she share in some of the expenses? And had, once, done this in a backhanded way. In 1598 she paid 1,120 crowns to Richard Staper and others as a reward for building 'three good ships'. But this was really because she needed as many ships as possible in case Spain attacked England again, which was constantly, and rightly, expected. Armed merchant ships had to serve with the navy in time of war (and still have to today). For now, however, she ignored the company's pleas.

Barton continued to press the council. Already, he wrote at the end of October 1595, the delay of the Venetian present was making Constantinople think the Doge was simply waiting to see how the Turkish war with the emperor would pan out. Then, to Barton's horror, a new Venetian *bailo* turned up – and with a present! [25]Among much else, a colossal silver-gilt model ship so heavy it required two men to carry it, as well as masses of the usual cloth-of-gold, velvet, taffeta, damask and satin. However horror was mitigated by relief – the Venetians had 'disgraced so rich a present' by including four great cartwheel-sized Parmesan cheeses – only for the relief to turn swiftly back to horror again: the Turks loved the cheeses! Then, Mehmed III planned to lead his army in person against the Holy Roman Emperor in the spring of 1596 and, as Barton pointed out unnecessarily to the Vice Chamberlain of the Privy Council, Sir Thomas Heneage, 'What trouble itt wilbe to follow him with sayed present yr Hon's wisdom may judge.'

But said present continued not to appear – or even to be prepared. On 6 December 1595, Richard Staper himself wrote to Robert Cecil asking him to intercede with the queen to get her to send a present.[26] He pointed out that the French king 'doth always supply the Present at his own whole charge which is £3000.' But Barton had unwisely let the queen know that Henry IV had still not accredited his own ambassador because his treasury was broke due to the French civil wars (exactly the sort of chaotic and bloody wars which the Ottoman constitution had evolved successfully to avoid.)

But at this point some of the merchants, at least, seem to have relaxed. Perhaps nothing had to be done at all – or nothing yet. Clearly Barton, with his charm, his contacts, and his skill, got on perfectly well accredited or not. But there was another, odder reason to relax. In March 1596, John Sanderson, in Aleppo but now the company's principal factor in Constantinople, wrote that there was no reason for a present till the end of the year, for then: '... by that time out of doubt somewhat will come to pass, either good or bad, for this empier ...' The reason was that there was a widespread belief, backed by prophesies and signs, that, since

Constantinople had been built by one Constantine and had been lost by another, it had been destined to fall to one Mehmed, as it had to Mehmed II, and be taken from another, Mehmed III, now on the throne. So general had the assumption become that by the end of the year, in September 1596, the Fugger agent in Rome sent this dispatch to his master in Augsburg: 'A flysheet will shortly be printed here announcing that the Ottoman Empire and Mehmed III ... will soon come to an end, and that Constantinople will fall into the hands of the Christians. This to happen in 1597 or a little later, in accordance with the forecasts of all Prophets and of Holy Writ, as well as of the Turks.' The fact that Mehmed had recently left to lead his troops against the Holy Roman Emperor somehow substantiated this.

[27]In fact, the empire was still at the height of its power, but from now on there were regular prophecies of the imminent decline and collapse of the Ottomans – often because they were all 'enfeebled with the continual converse of women'. One detects a note of envy there, and later.

Barton, quite rightly, believed none of it. He had decided to accompany Mehmed and fight for him, but even there he became more and more anxious about the non-arriving, non-*existent* present. In a letter of 29 September 1597, he wrote to Sanderson, who was about to return to Constantinople, 'We have so small comfort of the present. And I marville our friends in Aleppo doe not more diligently solicit the same, for there owne benefit and sortie of there trade, knowing our privileges be not yet confirmed. I cannot write to the company more than I have thereupon ... '

This sudden, and untypical, note of despair may have been due to ill health. Shortly afterwards, Barton unexpectedly died. He died of dysentery after a short illness. He was buried, as he had requested, in front of the Greek monastery on the island of Heybeli about twenty miles from Constantinople. The Fugger agent said 300 people attended his funeral, with many representatives of foreign states. The Sultan and the pashas all regretted his death because he was such a likeable man. He was thirty-four. (And he had, incidentally, still not paid the mufti back his £1,500.)

Barton's death appalled the Levant Company. It acted on them like a lash. They realised they had waited far too long. They should have sent a new present three years earlier before the danger became acute. The old capitulations had collapsed with the death of Murad, but they had continued to hold up largely because of the adroitness and prestige of Edward Barton, almost an ambassador despite not being an ambassador. Now they had no one.

Or virtually no one. Only a year before he died, Barton had asked the company to send him an assistant. They had sent out Henry Lello. He now took over, but unlike Barton, who had had seven or eight years to learn the Levant Company's business, Lello had had virtually no time at all. His character will emerge, but it was to have a considerable effect on the story as it developed.

In fact, the company had vaguely begun to get things together. In October 1598, Richard Staper had written to Sanderson, still hoping the queen would step in and help, that because her government, with good cause, was once again obsessed with Spain, 'the present is forgotten, and I feare it will be so this yeare, yet some cloth is alredie provided by their honours six months past, which they will kepe redie till they give orders for other things'.

They now abandoned all hope of the queen and gave orders immediately – orders for something so bizarre that only on close examination does it become comprehensible. This was for a church organ, of a sort extraordinary even in a country of church organs – made for a country where they didn't exist and which knew nothing about them. And the man they chose to make it, and to take the tremendous journey to the Court of the Ottoman Sultan, was a young, unknown Elizabethan craftsman – Thomas Dallam.

CHAPTER 2

The Mystery of Dallam and the Organ

1 – The discovery of the diary

But before we follow Dallam in this huge task and on his epic journey, there is a tricky problem to be faced – and, if possible, solved.

Dallam's story rests on two discoveries made in the mid-nineteenth century. The first was his handwritten diary, which was offered for sale to the British Museum in 1846 and bought in 1848. [28]It can now be found in the British Library and, if you can follow Dallam's (surprisingly good) Elizabethan handwriting, read. On the first page, the librarian of the time has written 'Purchased of Th (Mr) Rodes, 11 November 1848 from the Collection of Works of Art and Vertu, comprising pictures, books, prints and sculpture formed by Henry Rodes (1846).' This catalogue is now marked as 'Destroyed' and no one has since been able to find any trace of Rodes or his collection.

[29]The diary was published by the Hakluyt Society in 1893, transcribed, indeed almost translated, with notes, by Theodore Bent. The editing has been described as the work of a madman.[30] It isn't – but it is careless. For instance, Bent often omits Dallam's marginal additions, which are sometimes significant.

The diary is unique. Artisan or trade backgrounds had never been a bar to literary talent or success; famously Shakespeare's father was a glover, and Ben Jonson was the son of a bricklayer. Edmund Spencer was the son of a journeyman. But personal details of working-class men and women, until the nineteenth century, come entirely from what the rich and educated wrote about them (except perhaps in plays – Marlowe was the son of another tradesman, a Canterbury shoemaker). The diary form itself was not at all common, even among the upper educated class, until the middle to end of the seventeenth century. And those men who came from similar backgrounds to Dallam were professional writers, not craftsmen or artisans (though Ben Jonson did work for a while as a bricklayer, and hated it).

Unique, therefore, in several ways. However we can only gather a certain amount from Dallam's diary – the events he describes, his general views and a good deal about his character. But it is far harder to find out about him before the diary events, which later made him celebrated for a while. When was he born, for instance? It is this that gives rise to the first major problem about Dallam – was he actually the chief constructor of the organ at all? One historian, Greg Bak, has argued persuasively that he was not.

Everything seems to hang on Dallam's date of birth. [31]Stanley Mayes, who wrote the first, indeed so far only, book about him in 1956, assumed he was born in 1570, and almost certainly near the hamlet of Dallam near Warrington in Lancashire. This assumption, or speculation, was sound in 1956, especially as we know Dallam got married in 1601, which means he was by then established in his trade. For the Levant merchants to have spotted him, he must have been working in London. Mayes argued that he would have come to London between the ages of fourteen and sixteen. If sixteen, he would have arrived in London in 1586. He would have had to join a guild, both to learn his trade (the only way in an age without books or manuals of instruction), and to gain essential privileges, like having a workshop in the city, being able to stand for civic office, and above all to have the protection of a powerful trade body – it meant, for example, that he could be tried, judged and punished by freemen of his city. The organ builders' guild was dissolved in 1531, thereafter the guild members joined the Blacksmiths' Company.

Dallam would have taken seven years to become a journeyman (1593), and by 1599, the year we have now reached, he would be twenty-nine and have been a journeyman for six years (eight years if he had come south when fourteen). All this sounds appropriate for a young man who was to undertake such an important commission, ostensibly for the queen.

However, it is not as simple as Mayes was able to assume. After he had written his book, an entry of baptism was discovered in the registry of Flixton Parish Church, some way from Warrington. This referred to a Thomas Dallam son of Thomas Dallam – baptised 1 May 1575. [32]All subsequent writers, and there have been a good many, have taken this to be the Thomas Dallam of the diary – and it may be so.

[33]Assuming this, like all other writers, Greg Bak argues in an article titled 'Who built the organ for the Sultan?' that in fact Dallam was *not* the principal builder of the organ at all. Briefly, he points out that if he became an apprentice in 1589 at fourteen (the more usual age), he would have become a journeyman in 1596, and so, if the contract was made in 1597, as seems likely, he would have had only *one year* as a professional organ builder, and in 1599 have been just twenty-four – both with too little experience and too young to be a master builder in charge of such an important, expensive and, in effect, royal commission (the organ cost £550 – between a quarter and half a million today). He supports the idea that Dallam was not a journeyman till 1597 by the fact that he got married in 1601 and journeymen usually only married after three or four years,[34] when they had become householders.

Bak says that, essentially, Dallam was not the main architect but a junior figure, possibly in a team led by Edmund Schetz, court organ builder between 1587 and 1600. And he builds a powerful case. However, it is not unassailable.

When was Dallam Born?

There is no actual evidence that the 1575 Flixton Thomas Dallam was *our* Thomas Dallam. Saints' Christian names were extremely common in the sixteenth and seventeenth centuries. At Flixton between 1573 and 1575,

John was by far the most common name (twenty-four Johns), with Thomas (seven) coming next. And the name Dallam was so common in Lancashire then that there is still a street called Dallam Lane leading out of Warrington. In most of the relevant nearby parishes, records start too late, but there are ten Dallams recorded in the little parish church of Farnworth a few miles west of Warrington; [35]five more crop up in the record book of Warrington itself. [36]And it is odd that the list of 'worthies' in the Flixton parish history does not mention any Dallams, although after 1600 and throughout the seventeenth century, the Dallams were celebrated organ builders all over England and indeed into France.

[37]And there is some evidence, albeit shaky, that Dallam was born in 1570. The Jesus Christ Latter Day Saint's website, which specialises in searching out and publishing information from English parish registers, states unequivocally that Dallam was born in 1570, although they provided no conclusive evidence of this. Nevertheless, they also give the dates of Dallam's marriage and the birth of his children – and these are all correct.

And even if Dallam was only twenty-two at the time in 1597 that he was chosen as the chief figure to build the organ, this could easily be explained by the fact that there were very few organ builders at the end of the sixteenth century. The rise of the Puritans meant that many churches got rid of their organs and, in 1563, the Convocation of Canterbury, the church's governing body, failed by only one vote to have all of them destroyed. After this, dozens of organs were removed. Their pipes were melted down, mixed one-part lead to nine-parts tin, and sold as pewter. The resulting pewter plates and mugs are still common in junk shops and antique shops today. As a result, organ building became a dying craft. There were no new organs built at all between 1570 and 1579, and only one between 1580 and 1589. A single area of England retained a fondness for organs and that was the north-west, where Dallam was born. This was because the north-west remained strongly, if secretly, Catholic – [38]and it seems possible, though this is not certain, that Dallam was himself a recusant (concealed) Catholic.

It would seem that Bak's argument that Dallam couldn't have been the chief architect of the organ doesn't really stand up. But, in fact, I think the whole problem vanishes the moment we look closely at the second nineteenth century discovery which, as I mentioned earlier, underpins his story, and this was the discovery of part of the contract drawn up to commission the Levant Company's still seemingly eccentric gift.

Identity of Randolph Bull

[39]The contract, or this part of the contract, formed the substance of an article in the 20 October 1860 issue of *The Illustrated London News*. It is accompanied by an illustration which it is claimed was on parchment attached to the contract, though it looks to me suspiciously like a nineteenth century drawing based on details in the contract. Both originals have since vanished.

But the contract is extremely revealing. It is between 'Randolph Bull, citizen and goldsmith' on the one hand, and Richard Staper and the Levant Company merchants on the other. (Schetz isn't mentioned.) The said merchants desire to have 'a new instrument of extraordinary kind, and endowed with various motions, both musical and of special use, such as for rarity and art may render it fit to be sent from Her Majesty to any Prince or Potentate ...'

In the drawing and the contract, the figure of Her Majesty, set with forty-five jewels, including emeralds and rubies (like the real queen, in fact), had to hold a prominent place on the organ and move in various ways; the organ also had to include an angel which turned an hour glass every sixty minutes. The specification makes clear that the maker was allowed to alter the design as he thought fit, provided a proportion of the merchants also thought fit. Clearly they did think fit, and queen and angel were both dropped. Sensible moves. The glorification of the English queen on the main present to the Sultan would not have been tactful. And it is clear from Dallam's later description that the organ, while still sixteen feet high, was very different from the one in *The Illustrated London News*.

But it was not so different in those 'various motions'. It is these that reveal the main thrust of the gift. Once the queen and the angel had been jettisoned, six other motions remained: central was a great, round, 24-hour clock, which also showed the waxing and waning of the moon and the positions of the planets. (To the Ottomans, as to the rest of Europe, astrology was a major and vital science.) Below the clock, 'a great barrel with a chime of very tunable bells' would sound at the hour or when the director set it off. Above and to the left of the great clock, an armed man at a tower would strike the quarter hour 'upon a fine, loud and sounding bell'. Next, a second armed man at the opposite tower would strike the hour 'upon a greater bell'. Higher up, two trumpeters on either side would lift and sound their trumpets when the director set them off. And finally, at the very top, there was a cockerel which would crow loudly on the hour and be made to flutter its wings.

The clock and cockerel are the clues to what had happened. In 1583 the merchants, as we have seen, had been much struck by the extraordinary effect their present had had on Murad III. This present was a clock with numerous mechanical 'motions'. They had transmitted the Ottoman enthusiasm to Barton, to the extent that not long before he died, he had suggested the queen should give a clock in the shape of a cockerel, which she apparently had in her apartments. [40] And other observers had commented, one in a letter to Barton, on the fascination Murad and his court had with such novelties.

The merchants and Staper had decided to follow Barton's advice but be even more extreme. And this is borne out by the choice of Randolph Bull as the second chief party to the contract.

For some reason, historians writing about Dallam haven't gone very deeply into Bull. They have accepted that he was a goldsmith and assumed he was chosen because the organ was to have 300 ounces of silver and many jewels, probably at least the forty-five mentioned in the contract, included in its construction. Naturally, a goldsmith or jeweller would be required; it is likely, adds Mayes, Bull was jeweller to the queen.

Randolph (or Rainulph) Bull was certainly a member of the Goldsmiths' Company, but he was not a goldsmith himself.[41] He was a horologist – a maker of clocks. He joined the Goldsmiths' Company for the same reason Dallam joined the Blacksmiths' – his own company had been dissolved some years before. Nor was he an ordinary clockmaker – in July 1591 he was appointed clockmaker to the queen, an appointment confirmed when James came to the throne. There is a watch made by him in the British Museum today, and a watch which strikes made by him in the Mallet collection of the Ashmolean at Oxford.

Joint Makers

In effect, what the merchants had requested – and, as we shall see, got – was not so much an organ/clock as a clock/organ (plus a good many more mechanical tricks).

The question of Dallam's age we can leave open, since there is no firm evidence on it. I personally incline to his being in his late twenties, from the impression of assurance and confidence given by the diary. But the precise position of chief architect, which exercises Greg Bak, now becomes clear. The role was divided: the queen's clockmaker, Randolph Bull, designed and oversaw the mechanical clock effects; the organ itself was built by Dallam, though he certainly also understood some of the mechanical side. [42]Blacksmith/clockmakers made many of the clocks in the sixteenth century, and Dallam may well have had some acquaintance with clockmaking. But even the organ – on the face of it a standard late sixteenth-century model, with a single keyboard and no pedals or stops – was not in the least simple. The mechanism detailed in the contract is so complicated as to be barely followable: 'Several strong, forcible and artificial bellows ... Wheels and pinions ... which would drive everything for 6 hours.' It was an elaborate engine of springs and conduits, connecting clockwork, barrels and pipes, and keys which had to be able to move on their own – far more complicated than an ordinary organ. Dallam may have understood it, but he had to take an engineer – his 'ingener' – with him, a figure mentioned in none of his later contracts

It was clearly an extremely time-consuming task to make this object of 'an extraordinary kind'. Mayes goes into a long, detailed and intelligent discussion of just how long it took based around the contract, stating it had to be ready before St John's Day. It wouldn't be at all surprising if it were late – that is, after 24 June 1598. (In subsequent years, Dallam's organs often took a year to make, and this was not an ordinary organ.)

It not only took a long time to build, but it was also extremely expensive. Along with the other gifts, it cost the Levant Company, in today's terms, over half a million pounds.

In any event, in January 1599 Dallam dismantled the organ, packed it up (the packaging itself being another almost unique feature) and accompanied it to Whitehall to show it to the queen.[43]

To See the Queen

We can't be sure where Dallam left with the organ since we don't know where he lived in London, nor under what conditions. No Dallams show up in the lay subsidy rolls, described by Charles Nicholl in his excellent book about Shakespeare in Silver Street as the Elizabethan telephone directory. This is not surprising – the Rolls are by no means complete.

[44]Dallam's son Robert lived in Covent ('convent') Garden so it is possible his father lived there too. Not knowing precisely, we can't tell what route he took to Whitehall, but it was almost certainly by the Thames.

[45]London had a population of approximately 200,000. On the way to becoming one of the greatest cities the world had ever known, capital of the largest empire it is ever likely to know, it was already, in 1600, third among the five largest cities in Europe, yet still not as large as several provincial cities in Britain today (Manchester, well over 500,000; Birmingham, over a million). Although, unlike most European cities, London had avoided siege, it was still defined by its massive thirty-feet high London Wall, which

followed the three-mile Roman Wall and its seven main gateways (Aldgate, Bishopsgate, etc.). It was a great market, not a fortress, yet the fortress still dominated the minds of its citizens – it is noticeable in Dallam's diary how he always comments on the fortifications of the places he sees. Within these walls were crammed about 140,000 people, with 40,000 equally crowded (a good number in shanty dwellings) outside the walls. South of the river were theatres, bull- and bear-baiting, and brothels (legal, but had to be painted white).

The narrow, unpaved little streets, twisting between wooden houses packed with lodgers, and frequently slums, often stank, not so much from the sewage running down the middle and the pisspots emptied from upstairs windows, though of that certainly, but of the acrid tang of burning coal, of wood smoke from the many fires, of the smell of cows and sheep, from the slaughter houses and many butchers, and of pigs wandering freely – though these were encouraged because they ate the muck and excrement. Kites, which foreigners noticed walking 'quite tame', were unmolested for the same reason. There were to be no public toilets for several centuries, and not for nothing were streets called Piss Alley or Shit Lane. Mud, excrement, soot, slime and smuts – all these left names too: Deadman's Place, Dirty Alleys, Dirty Hills, Dirty Lanes and Foul Lanes.

The streets were noisy and could be dangerous. Noisy with traders advertising by horns and clappers, the barking of roaming packs of dogs, the crowing of cockerels and clucking of hens, the squealing and grunting of pigs, with bells pealing from over one hundred churches. The cries and the sight of gulls were more numerous then, as they swooped in after the rubbish and remains of food lying about. Only at night did the great city grow quiet. Although policing was fairly effective, danger still came from footpads and criminals, who were regularly executed on Tower Hill. (Children were noticed gathering up the blood which had poured 'through slits in the skafold', though why they should do this Ackroyd, who recorded the observation, does not say.) There had been a property boom when church lands and buildings were sold off, but many of these had been exempt from secular law and these exemptions continued. Warrens of criminals and debtors grew up, as at Coldharbour and St Martin's Le Grand.

Living in these conditions it is hardly surprising that Londoners died young. Life expectancy in the poorer parishes was 20–25 years; even in the rich it was 30–35 years. Plague carried off thousands, sweeping again and again in lethal waves across the city: in 1563, 17,000 died; in 1593 (when Dallam was probably living there), 18,000; in 1603, 30,000. Until 1780, deaths exceeded births and London's population only grew due to immigration from all over England and, to an extent, Europe. It has been estimated that one sixth of all Englishmen became Londoners in the second half of the sixteenth century.

If the little alleys and narrow streets were crowded and noisy, the bigger roads were not much better. The Strand, for instance, the main road towards Whitehall and Westminster through the village of Charing, was, as Parliament noted, 'full of pits and sloughs, very perilous ... very noyus and foul, and in many places thereof very jeapardous to all people ... ' And it, too, was deafening with drays, carts, horses and coaches, the drivers shouting and cursing, the iron-rimmed wheels clanging round on the cobbles. We forget that the car, when it eventually came, was welcomed as *quiet*.

It is likely, therefore, that Dallam accompanied the dismantled and packed-up organ on its journey up the Thames. This was, in fact, the main London thoroughfare. Scores of wherries plied up and down and across it, with sloops, barges, little ships of all sizes and descriptions so that the river seemed a forest of tossing masts and flapping sail. And we should note here that despite the rubbish dumped into it, and the sewage flowing into it and its tributaries like the River Fleet, the Thames was still relatively clean. Nearly all London's fish were caught there. 'What should speak of the fat and sweet salmon daily taken in the stream,' wrote Stow in 1598, 'and that in such plenty ... as no river in Europe is able to exceed it? But what store also of barbells, trouts, perches, smelts, bream, roaches, daces, gudgeon, flanders, shrimps, eels, etc. are commonly to be had therein?' And despite the poverty and discomfort, disease and crime, London was intensely alive, the population young and vigorous; and it was becoming increasingly prosperous. William Harrison, in his *Description of England (1587)*, quoted by Mayes, said that even 'inferior artificers' had bad plate (probably pewter from old recycled organ pipes), tapestries and silk hangings in their homes. The Levant merchants would hardly have had a market were this not so.

Dallam and his organ would have been rowed upstream to Whitehall. He could have been punted. The Thames, with its gravel course, was much wider and shallower then. Timber barges were punted up the river, as were rafts of logs. There were the marshes and mudflats, with seagulls gliding over them, of a tidal river. Proper islands appeared at low tide. (Battersea and Bermondsey commemorate old islands – 'ea' is Anglo-Saxon for island.)

And, of course, famously, the Thames regularly froze over, twenty-three times between 1620 and 1814 and at least eight times before that. Sometimes the ice was so thick Londoners held 'frost fairs' on it. Partly this was precisely because it was shallower (you could walk across it at low tide above Westminster), and partly because it was colder in the sixteenth century. The Little Ice Age lasted from about 1300 to 1850. The temperature was an average of two degrees Celsius lower, but 'average' meant it was sometimes very much lower than today (beggars were not infrequently found frozen to death in the streets). But the main reason the ice became so thick was because of London Bridge, begun in 1176. It was built on nineteen massive boat-shaped stone piers, with a road above lined with tall houses and the heads of executed traitors, boiled and stuck on spikes. These giant piers essentially dammed the river, leaving it calm above and so able to freeze. Underneath there were rapids, which could be dangerous – fifty watermen a year died trying to shoot them (and this was the reason young Osborne had proved so brave rescuing his master's baby – his future wife).

The bridge was demolished in 1831 – several years before the Victorians built up the embankments – and the river never froze again.

Once arrived at Whitehall, Dallam had to set the organ up in the banqueting hall. This was an unsteady edifice, hurriedly constructed in 1581 (it took 375 men three weeks and three days). [46]It was over ninety feet long and made of poles and canvas painted to look like stone, with 292 glass windows and decorated, according to Holinshed's *Chronicles,* with foliage hanging from the painted canvas ceiling and 'pomegranates, oranges, pompions [pumpkins] ... '[47] It was supposed to be temporary but, wrote another chronicler, 'with much propping it stood until the fourth yeare of King James'. Into this ramshackle building strode the queen – now fairly ramshackle herself, with her chamberlain and attendants there to inspect this object which, despite the pleading of the Levant Company and although she hadn't contributed a penny, was to go out in her name.[48]

Elizabeth at this time was sixty-six years old. M. de Maisse, the French ambassador, described her two years before:

[49]'Her dress had slashed sleeves lined with red taffeta, and was girt about with little sleeves that hung down to the ground, which she was forever twisting and untwisting. She kept the front of her dress open, and one could see the whole of her bosom, and passing low, and often she would open the front of her robe with her hands as if she were too hot ... Her bosom is somewhat wrinkled as well as one can see for the collar she wears round her neck, but lower down her flesh is exceeding white and delicate. As for her face, it is, and appears to be, very aged. It is long and thin, and her teeth are very yellow and unequal ... Many of them are missing ... '

Most observers described her teeth as black from eating too much sugar, like nearly all her adult subjects (bad breath was endemic). White skin was fashionable as proof you were not a labourer, just as tanned skin was fashionable three centuries later – until everyone had tanned skin – to show you could afford foreign holidays.

Maisse includes a summary of the jewels she was wearing, as do most contemporary accounts of her. Elizabeth loved jewellery. [50]An inventory of 1582 drawn up by Mrs Blanche Parry, retired gentlewoman of the bedchamber, lists 628 separate items. A portrait of Elizabeth in Hatfield House shows her covered in jewels: '...a great ceremonial collar composed of pearls in filigree interspersed with huge gems ... *The Three Brothers* hangs in the centre of the bodice ... ' *The Three Brothers* – three giant rose-red rubies set around a central pointed diamond, three round pearls and a ruby pear – had been acquired by Edward VI. [51]The scented jewellery of the Middle Ages continued into the sixteenth century. Mary Queen of Scots was executed wearing a chain of scented pomander beads from which hung a jewelled Agnus Dei.

And this love of display was not just feminine vanity. It was true all over Europe and round the Levant. Today, when male and female clothes are the most boring in the history of fashion, and have been for the last eighty years, it is hard to realise how important dress was to demonstrate rank and wealth and therefore power. And this for centuries. [52]In 1763, when Casanova, in London, was greeted with less respect than he expected by Mrs Cornelys, it is because he showed 'no sign of wealth on me ... all my diamonds were in my jewel case'. Jewellery was central to this demonstration, as we'll see again when Dallam arrives in the Ottoman court.

This jewel-loving queen was also clever. She spoke the three main European languages and could write and read Latin and Greek, and her mind was still sharp. And she had a temper. When irritated by her ministers she would throw her shoes at them.

The strange organ was clearly a surprise and a success. [53]John Chamberlain, who was at the presentation, wrote to Dudley Carleton, 'A great and curious present is going to the Grand Turk, which will scandalise other nations, especially the Germans.' Especially the Germans because they were still fighting the Turks. Elizabeth had already put Thomas Arundel under house arrest for helping the German emperor in this war.

And so, at last, as the new head of the Levant Company in Constantinople, Henry Lello, was becoming desperate with anxiety and impatience, the organ was ready for its long, difficult and dangerous journey, over 5,000 miles east, to the Sultan and the centre of the most powerful and richest empire in the West at that time – the great Ottoman Empire.

One person, however, was not ready: Thomas Dallam.

CHAPTER 3

The Voyage Out

A Fearful Storm

The first two lines of Dallam's diary state immediately that he was only told at the last moment – 'upon verrie short warninge' – that he himself was expected to make the colossal journey out to Constantinople with the organ. And he follows this with a long list (thirty-seven items) of what he bought for the expedition, noting particularly what each cost him: nine shirts (£2.12s.0d); two suits (£3.0s.0d), one of tough sackcloth to wear at sea; two waistcoats (16/-); a dozen handkerchiefs (10/-); three pairs of shoes (7/-) ... He had clearly been warned that the voyage out might take six months or more; with the voyage back, he would be away well over a year.

Among much else, he took in addition a small spinet, a sword, two knives and thirty pounds of tin and a gross of tin spoons, showing he expected the organ, or at least its pipes, would suffer some damage on the journey. The tin and spoons added a further £1.7s.0d to his expenditure. In all, he disbursed nearly £20 – a considerable sum when you realise a skilled artisan would have earned about £30 a year. [54]Dallam had presumably just been paid his share for finishing and delivering the organ, but clearly he knew he'd be paid back, which must be why he noted all the prices so precisely.

He was also not unnaturally worried about the shipboard diet, which was notorious at the time. [55]Mayes quotes Tom Nash, the pamphleteer, hearing sailors who talk 'of nothing but eating tallow and young blackamores [meeting, presumably, not eating], of five and five to a rat in every mess and the ship boy to the tail, of stopping their noses when they drank stinking water that came out of the sump of the ship, and cutting a greasy buff jerkin in strips and boiling it for their dinner'.

To alleviate this, he took a cordial, *Rose Solis,* along with oil, vinegar, prunes, cloves, mace, pepper, nutmegs, oatmeal, two pounds of sugar and also raisins – even though raisins and currants would soon be coming out of his ears. These were as popular and as common as peanuts now and were one of the chief imports of the Levant Company.

The organ, dismantled and in crates, had been sent down river to Gravesend. Dallam followed soon after, first rowing the considerable distance to Blackwall (paying 1/6) with his 'Chiste' full of his purchases, before transferring to a second boat in which he was rowed to Gravesend (6d), arriving at his ship the *Hector* on 9 February 1599.

His cabin, which he probably shared with three companions, who we'll meet in a moment, had not yet been assigned. Indeed, nothing was ready, though the crates holding the organ had been stowed near an elaborate and ornate coach secured to the spars, a present for the queen mother (the valide), a significant figure in the Ottoman court.

Dallam found lodgings in Gravesend for four days (3/- a day), and rejoined the *Hector* again on 13 February. There was a fair wind from the east and they set sail that very afternoon, only to anchor again at Deal for another four days when the wind dropped. Dallam – gregarious, humorous, enterprising and clearly popular – went ashore with the crew and others 'to make ourselves merrie'. Too merrie in one instance. When the wind picked up, and had to be grabbed, it was during the fourth night. A sailor came from the ship and went round the brothels and taverns summoning them all back. One of the five trumpeters, who were used for communications between ships, refused to come, yelling insults from his locked room. We 'left that Dronkerd be hinde,' wrote Dallam, and they hurried back to the ship.

The *Hector*, at 300 tons, had been commissioned and chartered by the Levant Company and was one of the largest merchantmen afloat (but not by any means one of the largest ships. Some of the five or six 'queen's ships' –the embryonic navy – were 1,000 or 1,500 tons).[56] But these little wooden Elizabethan sailing ships could go anywhere. Drake's *Golden Hind*, only 100 tons, went round the world. But they depended, naturally, on the winds – and could be at their mercy.

The Little Ice Age didn't increase the severity of the storms in the Channel, (though the cold -and Dallam notes how cold it was – made the storms, when they came, more unpleasant), but it must have made the thick fogs which would hide jagged rocks even denser and even more terrifying. And both storms and fogs could be. In September 1583 the *Golden Hind*, returning to England, ran into 'terrible seas ... men which all threw [their] lifetime had occupied the sea, never saw more outrageous seas'.[57] An accompanying 10-ton pinnace was completely 'devoured and swallowed up', and a few years before the *Hector* sailed, a Captain Glenham had been trapped in Dartmouth for two months by storms.

Thirty miles or so out from Deal, the *Hector* was suddenly struck by one of these great storms, and was then enveloped in dense fog. For two days, the ship was swept down the Channel out towards the Atlantic, completely lost. How far they were swept is difficult to ascertain from Dallam. When the fog lifted a little, the sailors told him they were nearing Ireland, which seems too far; Theodore Bent, the Hakluyt editor of Dallam's diary, has them near the Channel Isles, which doesn't seem far enough. At any event, the wind dropped sufficiently for Richard Parsons, the captain and a formidable figure, to start the *Hector*'s slow battle back to land. The fog, however, was once again very thick. At the end of the third day of the dying storm they saw, all at once, right ahead, too near to avoid, huge waves breaking against 'Verrie greate Rockes'. It was clearly frightening – sailors shouting, the crashing waves suddenly audible, the wind still high in the rigging – but [58]'it pleased almyghtie God ... to defend us from harme'. The ship had managed to get opposite Dartmouth harbour. The rocks marked its entrance. They sailed through – and were safe.

Clearly frightening – but also, to Dallam at least, very exciting as well as very strange. But it wasn't over. Within a few days they were in danger again.

Pirates

The *Hector* had been accompanied by a pinnace, the *Lanneret* (a hawk), a much smaller vessel which was to go with them, for its own protection, as near as possible to Venice. The pinnace had vanished in the storm, but they now learnt that, having lost its main mast and being attacked by four Dunkirkers,[59] it had fled to Falmouth. They now sent word to Captain Parsons that they would meet up with him at Plymouth. This they did, but once again the wind changed and both ships had to spend a further seven days in port.

They set out again on 16 March 1599, only to be stopped by an urgent trumpet signal from a caravel.[60] Two of the boat's sailors came aboard with an urgent warning. They had been sailing on a warship, the *Plow*, but had been stopped by Dunkirkers – seven ships this time – and closely questioned as to the whereabouts of the *Hector*. They said they 'had never hard of suche a shipp', upon which the Dunkirkers had killed a number of them, taken the *Plow*, and set six of the men loose in the caravel.

There are three things we can learn from this. There was no such thing as 'security' at that time. The news that the *Hector* was carrying expensive presents to the Sultan had clearly leaked out more or less at once: it was probably known at various places all the way to Constantinople. It was certainly known in Algiers when they reached there.

The second significant point is the anarchy which reigned on the high seas then. The Dunkirkers were pirates – or more likely privateers, though in practice there was little difference. 'Privateers' were ships engaged in piracy who were supposed to have permission from their sovereign. Every nation regarded reprisals at sea as a legitimate way of carrying on a war or of redressing wrongs done to them *in the past*. In this case, the war being carried on was the one against Spain. But English ships, which often had unscrupulous captains, and were never checked, seemed to regard almost any foreign ship as fair game, as witness their predatory names – *Dragon, Lion, Panther, Ferret, Tiger*. One was simply called *Why Not?*

The reason was money. National privateering, or piracy, was very paying both to the ships and the nation. Fifteen per cent of England's imported income came from privateering. For example, in 1580, Drake brought back booty worth £600,000. The queen's share was £160,000 – almost what she got a year. She paid off all her debts and invested, as we saw, £40,000 in the Levant project.

The Dunkirkers now threatening the Channel could pose as Spanish privateers (or French). They were led by Simon de Danser, a Dutchman from Doordrecht, with a crew of ruffians of several nationalities. In 1598, six of these ships had led Viking-like plundering raids on the coasts of Norfolk and Suffolk; in 1583 they had actually captured Yarmouth for a while.

They were, that is, ruthless, dangerous, numerous and well armed, and the two men from the caravel warned Captain Parsons not to sail 'with oute good store of companye'. Parsons would have none of it. 'He would not staye one hour for any more companye than God alreddie had sent him', which was the *Lanneret* and two other small ships going to Newfoundland and needing protection till out of the Channel.

[61]And this is the third significant point this incident reveals – the enormous power of the *Hector*. There was, in fact, not a great deal of difference between a big man-of-war under the crown and an armed merchantman. The ships of the crown were bigger. The *Revenge*, for instance, carried forty-three guns, the *Hector* had twenty-seven, with space for more, and the armament was formidable. The favourite weapon of the navy then was the culverin. This was developed in England in 1543 for land warfare but was swiftly adapted for ships, usually by shortening the barrel. Culverins were made of cast iron. Bronze was better, but cast iron was a third or quarter cheaper. The

only drawback to cast iron was that the guns could and often did burst; but with both bronze and cast iron there was a further danger. The gunpowder cartridge could explode if loaded into too hot a barrel with, as the *Hector* was to discover in Constantinople, horrifying consequences. Half of her guns were demi-culverins – barrel length twelve feet, but on ships usually eight or nine feet; weight of shot – 9.9 lbs; range theoretically a mile, but they were usually fired point-blank at about 400 feet, where the effect was devastating. A nine-pound shot could smash through three or four feet of solid seasoned oak. Each demi-culverin weighed 3,000–3,400 lbs and they were carried low in the ship to avoid destabilising.

The remainder of the *Hector*'s armoury consisted of culverins of descending weight and power. Sakers, with six-foot long barrels, shot of five to seven pounds, the gun weighing about 1,800 lbs; and minions – smaller but not all that small – with barrels five feet or so, shot three to four pounds, weight of gun 1,200 lbs. This tremendous firepower meant that armed merchantmen were enjoined to fight for the crown when needed, which they still are. During the Second World War my father, a doctor in the navy, served on HMS *Carinthia*, an armed merchant cruiser helping guard the convoys in the North Atlantic. The *Carinthia* was sunk, but the whole crew was saved. But this use by the nation of armed merchant ships was the reason that in 1598 the queen, as we saw, had paid 120 Crowns to Staper and others for building their ships. Of the 197 ships that fought the Armada, only thirty-four were truly crown ships, 163 were armed merchantmen. It also meant Captain Parsons was totally confident that, if it came to it, he could dominate and, if necessary, destroy any Dunkirkers who tried to come against him.

It did come to it. That same day, 16 March 1599, the *Hector* sailed. The early spring wind was fresh and very cold, whipping the tops of the waves and humming in the rigging. The *Lanneret* tried to follow but 'our ship sayled so well that we could spare the pinis our main saile' and it was soon left behind. ('Spare our mayne saile' – Dallam more and more shows how much he talked to and learnt from the crew and others on the *Hector*.)

Early next morning, their look-out spotted three ships bearing towards them, followed by four more. It was the Dunkirkers. All the company's ships were built for speed to take cargo to and from the Levant as quickly as possible. The *Hector* could easily have escaped. Instead, Parsons ordered the big guns to be made ready and distributed arms to crew and passengers. Dallam had a 'muskett' added to his sword. Then the *Hector* went about and sailed back towards the pursuing Dunkirkers.

Neither side at first looked likely to give way. But when there was half a mile between them, Parsons had the *Hector* turned broadside to the still advancing Dunkirkers. He hoped, Dallam was told, that at the sight of his firepower they would think they were one of the queen's ships (which shows incidentally, that the *Hector* had watertight gun ports, new invented, something confirmed later in a letter Lello wrote to Sir Robert Cecil).[62]

This clearly happened. At the sight of the *Hector*'s full size revealed side-on, her gun ports and armed men on her decks, the Dunkirkers went about and fled. Now it was the *Hector*'s turn to pursue, and she soon came up with them. It took three warning shots (Dallam hearing for the first time the exhilarating sound of the exploding gunpowder cartridges), the last cannon ball cutting through the largest Dunkirker's mainsail, before they obeyed the bosun's yelled command to heave-to.

Eventually, three of the Dunkirker captains came aboard the *Hector*. 'One of our company,' noted Dallam, 'saw one of them have under his arme a good long money bage full of somethinge, and so they went with the Mr [Captain] ... into his cabin.' They stayed there two or more hours, eventually emerging behind Parsons, who called the whole ship's company before him and read out a letter 'which seemed to be but newly wrytten' purporting to be a pass from the King of France allowing the Dunkirkers to carry 'Sartyne wynes' which they had on their ships. This was not only blatantly untrue, it was proved so by some of the *Hector*'s men who had taken the time to go over some of the Dunkirker's ships and found nothing but weaponry.

Nevertheless, Captain Parsons, although obviously prompted by a large bribe, at once let the Dunkirkers go. There was a good deal of angry muttering from the crew, who would by custom have shared out one third the value of the captured ships. But there was nothing they, or anyone, could do. Captain Parsons was a formidable figure and they were frightened of him, with good reason. [63]The power of a ship's captain was total, over his crew more or less life and death, but over passengers, too. [64]A Captain Horne in charge of a trading voyage to South America had a row with one of the merchants on board. Horne had him tied to the mast with a full chamber pot round his neck.

It was not just the crew who was angry. From now on Dallam took against Parsons, stood up to him, something he proved a number of times on this expedition that he was perfectly capable of doing, and had several exchanges with him. He noted in the margin of his diary that the Dunkirkers subsequently attacked and terrorised shipping as far north as Newcastle, as was substantiated by the State Papers of the time.[65]

Captain Parsons, clearly infuriated by his sailors trying to explain that he was mistaken, ignored them. He ignored any angry muttering. He simply ordered the *Hector* to continue on course and make for Gibraltar as fast as possible.

The Mediterranean

As they speed south, it is interesting to look briefly at the conditions under which Dallam was living.

He himself hardly ever comments on these, from which one can deduce they can't have been too terrible – or too unlike what he was used to. In some respects they were probably better. A privie in most of the little wooden London houses was usually a plank with a hole over a shallow pit. [66]Even the best, regularly emptied, stank. [67]Many ships had tubs between decks, or hogsheads secured to the sides for 'the mariners to piss into that they may always be full of urine to quench fire with two or three pieces of old sail ready to wet in the piss'. It was much quicker to do this, apparently, than the lowering of endless buckets over the side. A 'necessary' seat was rigged up in the bulkhead venting over the sea.

Food on board ships was, as we saw, notoriously bad. Dallam doesn't mention it, though it may be significant that he always describes how they go ashore for fresh supplies and expresses disappointment if all they get is, for example, 'a bushel of garlicke'.[68]

Nor does he mention his accommodation, beyond indicating earlier that he had been promised a cabin. It is difficult to find any detailed contemporary descriptions of merchant ships of *Hector*'s class. [69]However, a ship very like *Hector* has been analysed by the Danish scholar Kristoff Glamann. The *Ceulen* plying the eastern trade not long after 1600 was also 300 tons, carried forty guns, a few more than the *Hector,* and had a crew of 105 with thirty soldiers. Plying the same route in 1613, the *Hector* had a crew of 100. The accommodation on the *Ceulen* for officers and important passengers was apparently 'adequate'.

Dallam was a craftsman, and socially not the equal of the Levant merchants also travelling; but he was also, as the man responsible for and in charge of the queen's present to the Sultan – the main reason for the entire voyage – the most important person on the boat: something Parsons, to his chagrin, was several times forced to acknowledge. Dallam probably shared his cabin with two or three of his mates.

These were his 'Ingener' John Harvey, Michael Watson (a joiner) and Rowland Buckett (a painter). [70]Mayes speculates that these men were all part of his business as a maker of organs, which is possible – but his Ingener, clearly essential for the complexities of this particular and unique organ, is never mentioned again in subsequent construction details, as I noted earlier, and Buckett, though he was to collaborate with Dallam once more, gained real distinction later as an independent operator. It took five years for Dallam to get going on his return. I think it more likely that he worked to setting up his business proper after his return, rather than before he set out.

Other figures of Dallam's class on the voyage included a cook and underbutler for Henry Lello's embassy and a coachman, Ned Hall, for the valide's coach. Dallam made friends with Hall as well.

[71]As to how he passed his time, Mayes has him playing his virginals and singing popular songs of the day like 'Watkin's Ale' or 'Whoops! Do me no harm, good man', which seems likely enough. But above all he observed, fascinated, the extraordinary things he saw, and what he observed he wrote down.

[72]The actual manuscript diary has 156 pages, is 19 cm long and 13.5 cm wide, with approximately thirty lines to a page when full (as most of them are) and about ten words to a line. The spelling is like all Elizabethan spelling – idiosyncratic – but the handwriting is good, if not quite as good as my only other experience of Elizabethan handwriting, the lay subsidy rolls, records of taxation in England between the twelfth and seventeenth centuries – but these were written by practised clerks. It was mostly written on the voyage, if sometimes a little after the events it describes, since up to 'Carthage', having so far written on one side of the page only, he changes to both sides, evidently realising he would run out of paper. There are numerous small insertions obviously made on the voyage, usually in the margin. But he often says he'll expand incidents (usually rows with Parsons or, later, Henry Lello) when he gets back. Some things he did add in England, like noting how the Dunkirkers let free by Parsons had sailed up the east coast doing further damage, or listing objects he had brought back to London.

Whether he ever wrote another, longer version, it is impossible to say, though it is conceivable. [73]But I somehow doubt it, and for the same reason, explained in the notes, that I don't think it surprising he doesn't seem to have tried to get it published. Dallam probably kept this record for his family.

If the handwriting is good, the prose itself is even better – straightforward, humorous, honest, vivid, even poetic at times, and original. [74]It has been commented on before: Stephen Bicknell, for instance, in his *History of the English Organ,* singled out Dallam's description, fruit no doubt of his early training, of lightning in a storm, 'lyke a verrie hote iron taken out of a smyth's forge, sometimes in liknes of a roninge worme, another time lyke a horshow and agine lyke a lege and foute'. I particularly liked Dallam's use of 'snufflinge' when, halfway through his enormous journey, the ship came to Scanderoon.

And as Dallam kept his notes, the *Hector* sped south, until 23 March when they were suddenly becalmed again. The next day an 'Infinite company of porposis' surrounded the ship, 'which did leape and Rone [run] marvellously'. A day later, they saw two or three 'Monstrus fishes or whales, the which did spoute water up into the eayere, lyke as smoke dothe ascend out of a chimney'.

The wind picked up and the *Hector* hurried on, and by 27 March was passing through the Straits of Gibraltar. This was a nervous moment. Gibraltar was full of Spanish galleys and men-of-war, and England was still at war with Spain – who was in fact actually planning another invasion attempt, which led, in a few months' time, to terrifying rumours sweeping the country with some near-farcical results.

They had left Plymouth on 16 March; with a day dealing with the Dunkirkers, and two days becalmed, they had reached the Mediterranean in about eight days – rapid sailing. But what astonished Dallam was that it had been very cold when they set out and it was now 'exsedinge hoote'. And spring had preceded them. Leaving Gibraltar behind, after he had noted how well fortified it was, he exclaimed at the greenery along the Spanish shore, the 'tres full blowne'.

They passed Marbella and Malaga ('Malligan'), and then Dallam saw gleaming in the far distance the perpetual snows of the 'hudg mountaynes' of the Sierra Nevada. Parsons turned the *Hector* south-east and on 30 March they anchored outside Algiers.

Algiers

[75]Algiers at this time was an intimidating place. It had been for many years what we could call the capital of piracy. Essentially, the whole of the

southern Mediterranean from Egypt to the Pillars of Hercules opposite Gibraltar was considered the Barbary Coast. ('Barbary' from the tribal name of the Berbers.) But piracy, as mentioned earlier, had dominated that sea for well over 100 years. A huge impetus came from the expulsion of the Moors from Spain. Proud, civilised, now warlike, with countries too poor to support or assimilate them, many thousands of traders, farmers, and merchants, furious at the loss of their property, were forced to take to piracy. Apart from needing to live, they were ferociously anti-Christian and wanted revenge.

But in fact pirates came from every nationality and were often Christians themselves who had been captured and 'turned Turk' – i.e. become Muslims. Not surprisingly. Their captors could be very brutal, especially – and that is why its reputation was so intimidating – in Algiers. Castration was the least of the things persuading the captured sailors and their passengers to become Muslim. The King of Algiers in the 1580s (known variously as 'King,' 'Bey,' 'Pasha' – Gosse, an authority, calls the ruler the Beglerby) had as his treasurer and chief eunuch Assan Agha. Assan was in fact the son of Francis Rowlie of Bristol, who had been captured from the *Swallow*.

Terrible tortures could be inflicted on captives; knotted cords twisted round heads, needles pushed under fingernails, feet roasted over fires. The King of Algeria in the 1590s was particularly sadistic and his torturers had devised a system of tying and trussing his victims so that when dropped from a moderate height every bone in their body was broken.

The numbers of prisoners/slaves involved was very large indeed. Thousands of them, mostly Spanish, built the mole which still protects the town. At one time it was estimated that there were 20,000 prisoners and so many were English that Easter collections were made in every parish church to pay their ransom. (One of the Spanish prisoners in the 1570s was Cervantes, captured after being wounded at Lepanto and imprisoned in Algiers for five years, 'fettered and manacled and threatened with death by impalement' until a ransom of 500 ducats was paid).

Naturally enough, this outrageous and lawless behaviour infuriated all the countries affected, and on 19 October 1541 an enormous expedition, mostly furnished by Spain, set out to get Algiers. It consisted of 500 ships and 12,000 sailors and soldiers, far larger than the Armada of 1588 – but, like the Armada, it was defeated by a storm. So many men were captured that the slave economy of Algiers collapsed and the price fell to an onion a slave. From then on, the pirates were more or less supreme, living off loot and ransoms.

They were able to reach this happy position because they enjoyed the tacit support of many of the rulers round the Mediterranean coast. Along the whole southern coast this was the Ottoman Sultan. In 1538, Barbarossa, then the legendary ruler of Algiers, captured 400,000 pieces of gold, 1,000 girls and 1,500 boys in raids on Tunis and up the Adriatic. Judiciously, he sent a gift of 200 boys bearing gold and silver and rolls of fine cloths to the then Sultan, Suleyman I, the Magnificent. (One notes boys, not girls.) He was made Admiral of Suleyman's fleet, and from then on pirates paid ten percent of their takings to every ruler prepared to leave them alone. After 1586, the Algerians seemed to have reluctantly, and intermittently, respected the Turkey and Levant Companies' agreements with the Ottoman sultans and from then on left English ships more or less alone. Even so, between 1610 and 1620, 150 English ships were held, if only temporarily, in Algiers.

The brutality of both pirates and the Turks, their unreliability towards English shipping and the reputation of Algiers were all well known at the time. Pirates, along with Turks, feature in various plays of the period. In early Shakespeare, for instance, or in Marlowe's *Tamberlain the Great* (ostensibly a fourteenth-century figure but clearly contemporary).

'Those Christians captives, which you keep as slaves.
Burdening their bodies with your heavy chains ...
That naked row about the Terrene sea.'

Dallam would have known this in a rough, probably exaggerated way, and have had other details supplied to him by *Hector*'s crew. It therefore required courage to venture into the town in 1599, which he did soon after they anchored.

Parsons Imprisoned

Dallam's first experience of Africa was extremely vivid and so are his observations. Algiers was built, like most Berber villages and towns (and like a few old villages in Andalucía today) in a series of interconnected, drab grey boxes as if made by insects, so close together, Dallam wrote, that 'a man beinge on top of one house may go over the greatest part of the towne'.

Three or four companions went with him, including Mr Chancie (Chauncey), the ship's doctor. They walked two or three miles into the countryside so that the physician could gather medicinal herbs and roots. Under the blazing sun it was again extremely hot and, returning, they were soon assaulted by the smells and deafening clamour of a north African market town, the steep, rocky and extremely narrow streets, filled with a jostling noisy crowd of animals and people – Turks, Jews, renegade Christians, many Spaniards and Italians, oxen, camels and 'diverse Moores com in riding, all naked, saving a little cloth before them like a childe's apron'. In addition he noticed the women – apparently thought to 'have no souls' – going with covered faces. He and his companions were also buying provisions for themselves: Dallam notes how cheap everything seemed to be – a 'partridge for less than one pennye and 3 quales at the same price'.

Another thing he observed was the ingenious way in which 'henes and chickins ... [were] hatchet by artificiall meanes, in stoves or hote houses, without the help of a hen', and this is the first time he says he will write a more detailed account 'heareafter ... yf God permitte'.

This system of incubation, ubiquitous round the southern Mediterranean coast, fascinated many travellers in the seventeenth century. George Sandys, among others, who toured the Middle East in 1610, has left an account of how it operated in Cairo, in his *A Relation of a Journey.*[76]

'In a narrow entry,' he wrote, 'on each side two rowes of Ovens, one over another.' On the lower floor were laid 'affals of flaxe', upon this were mats, and upon the mats, eggs – 6,000 of them. In the top ovens, separated from the lower by gratings, was burnt 'the dry and pulverated dung of camels, Buffoloes etc ... which giveth a smothering heat without visible fire'. The eggs stay in the bottom ovens for '8 dayes, turned daily', the heat kept moderate. They are then looked at against a lamp to see if embryos are developing, where two thirds are rejected. The smouldering fire is put out and the rest of the eggs transferred to the top ovens and left for ten days, after the ovens have been sealed. 'This they practise from the beginning of January until the midst of June, the Egges being most fit for that purpose.' Dallam had arrived bang in the middle of peak hatching season.

He and his companions returned to relax in the comparative cool and quiet of the *Hector*. But the next day, Parsons was summoned to the palace. The king wanted to see the present destined for the Sultan. Parsons explained it was too complicated a gift and would take too long to assemble, whereupon the king refused to let him go. Parsons was compelled to send for Dallam and Harvey to corroborate his story. This they did and only then was Parsons finally released. The *Hector* finished stocking up with fresh provisions and fresh water and on 4 April 1599, left Algiers *en route* for Malta and Sicily.

Sicily, Mt. Etna

For a while, they sailed east along the coast of Africa, passing Dellys and Bejaia (Bousie) where the sailors told Dallam St Augustine had had a school. On 7 April, Easter Eve, they ran into a sudden dramatic storm, with deafening claps of thunder and extraordinary lightning flashing down from the sky. Dallam's prose, as not infrequently, became vivid and almost poetic – harking back to his early training with a blacksmith. 'It was verrie wonderful and strainge,' he wrote in a passage I quoted earlier but which is worth quoting again, 'for we myghte se the eayre open and a fier lyke a verrie hote iron taken out of a smythe's forge, somtimes in liknes of a roninge worme, another time lyke a horseshow, and agine lyke a lege and a foute.'

They passed the site where Carthage had once stood (and Dallam, as I noted, changed to writing on both sides of his paper), on past Tunis and Cape Bon 200 miles into the Mediterranean, aiming between Sicily and Malta, but closer to Sicily. So close that by 15 April they could see, by day, the snows of Mount Etna glistening in the sun and by night 'manye flashis of fiere'.

Here, once again, they felt they were in considerable danger. Sicily was in the hands of Spain and her ports full of galleys and men-of-war – twenty or more according to Dallam.

Actually, the danger at this point was illusory. The Spaniards on Sicily were preoccupied with rumours of an imminent attack by the Turks. [77]The Fugger agent in Rome had reported that in Messina it was known that the Sultan was sending 200 ships there, with an additional twenty-five supplied by Elizabeth. But the rumour itself was an illusion. Turkey was short of money, timber and other necessary supplies. It had no intention of risking an attack like that. But it served the same purpose – tying up the Spaniards in needless expense and time – to foment the rumour.

In that age of very slow and often unreliable communications, rumour could be as important and influential as the truth. In fact, for this reason it is perhaps worth digressing briefly into one of these rumours about to engulf England, since it gives us insight into the anxieties that clearly affected Dallam and everyone else on the *Hector*.

Return of the Armada

No one in England believed that the defeat of the Armada in 1588 was the end of it. Nor did anyone in Spain, most of whom thought the defeat had been a fluke.

On 24 July 1599, Secretary of State Robert Cecil received news of a large build-up of Spanish forces, some 100 ships, reported to be about to head for

England, probably via Ireland. This was not the first of such reports. There had been similar ones in May 1591, October 1595, '96 and '97.

But the reports in 1599 were more serious, and quite soon rumour made them much more serious still. It was said that Philip III would lead the invasion himself. He had apparently declared that he would make his little finger lie heavier on England than his father's entire body. Two noblemen who had tried to make him change his mind were executed on the spot.

The idea was that his forces would come, not via Ireland, but hugging the French coast, then cross over and sail up the Thames. The city was ordered to equip and supply sixteen of its most powerful merchant ships to defend the estuary. Ten thousand men were to be called up in London. Letters were sent to bishops and clergy in the Home Counties advising them to expect an invasion within fifteen days.

Commanders were hurriedly appointed. Lord Thomas Howard made admiral; Sir Walter Raleigh – vice admiral; Mr Fulke Greville – rear admiral. Sir Thomas Gerard was made colonel of the Londoners, but was rejected by the city and the Earl of Cumberland appointed instead. Now responsible for the defence of the city, he had a brilliant idea – a barricade of boats across the river at Gravesend, which he would personally command with 1,500 musketeers.

On 6 August the Spaniards were reported to have landed on the Isle of Wight and at Southampton. There was panic – 'unwarranted fear and consternation in London,' wrote a contemporary, 'with such a cry of women, chaining of streets and shutting of gates as though the enemy had been at Blackwall.'

As fear grew, so the reports galloping into London became wilder and wilder. The Spaniards now had 200 ships and 50,000 men. The King of Denmark was sending a further 100 ships. The King of Scotland had raised 40,000 troops and the Spaniards planned to put him on the throne.

The plan for the barricade at Gravesend was now seen as not bold enough and an even bolder scheme was proposed. This was to immediately sink a line of hulks in the Thames channel. Soundings were taken near Barking Shelf and it was estimated eighty-three ships would have to be sunk, costing £25,000. As this idea itself sunk in, there was furious opposition. If the river were dammed like this, thousands of acres of farmland and marsh would be drowned, costing at least £40,000. The hulks would have to be loaded with rocks and other ballast. It would be impossible to raise them. The Thames would be permanently blocked and the trade of the city destroyed.

On Sunday, 12 August, all the commanders dined with the lord mayor to discuss the situation. The Spanish fleet was reported to be at Brest. And there was an even graver rumour. The queen was seriously ill, possibly already dead.

After ten days, the enemy still hadn't appeared. The call-up was stopped. Those already mustered were sent home, though put on an hour's notice to return. Price controls were issued on all main foods and on drink.

There was a final blaze of rumour starting late on 25 August. The Spanish fleet had been seen off the French coast. Once again, the lord mayor was instructed to call out all his men. At six o'clock on the morning of 26 August, 3,000 trained men were stationed in the streets. They stood hanging about for two hours, at which point a heavy shower of rain soaked them to the skin and they were sent home. Next morning, 30,000 citizens went out to Mile End and trained all day. This went on for a week. Then a report arrived that the Spanish fleet had been seen off the Azores. Gradually, the whole scare died away.

This farcical episode resulted in scandal. It showed how unprepared the country was for invasion. It would have been defeated at the first thrust. The victuals in the queen's navy were so rotten the sailors would have succumbed to food poisoning within days.

Yet, farcical? Perhaps. But the Spaniards had launched actual raids, on Ireland, for instance, on 17 March 1596; and two Spanish ships were driven ashore in Wales in November 1597. Rumours of this sort continued into 1601.

Rumour, superstition and irrationality always arise at times of fear (and the fears then, or rather the reasons for them, were very real). The peak time in England for witches and witch-burning was just after the Armada. And in 1939–40, England was swept by rumours that the Russians were invading. You could tell they were Russians by the snow on their boots.

Zante

Fear of the Spanish was further manifested on the *Hector* as they passed above Malta. Dallam was told, by other members of the crew, that this, too, was Spanish.

[78]In fact, it was ruled by the Knights of St John, though it was true it had been given to them by Charles V of Spain in 1530 when they had been driven from Rhodes by the Ottomans. They took their revenge, and from then on lived lives of chastity, piety, charity and by plundering any Muslim shipping that came within reach. This so maddened the Sultan that in 1565 a huge fleet, led by the Ottoman navy, sailed against Malta from Algiers. The island was besieged for six months and was about to capitulate when the Turks suddenly fled. News had come of a Spanish fleet sailing to the rescue. It was not true. The power of rumour was demonstrated once again.

And it is now, 15 April 1599, that Captain Parsons once more cheated on his crew (it was this, not his casual piracy, that irritated Dallam). They chased a small ship which, seeing their flag and more importantly their strength, hove to and sent its captain aboard with numerous valuable gifts, including 'tow or thre great peecis of salte fishe that wear 7 or 8 foute longe and one foute square. It was strainge fishe unto us'. Strange – but, alas, not to be tasted. After another large bribe, Parsons told the captain to go, taking all his presents. He explained this further example of blatant behaviour by saying that the ship came from Chios, and had been authorised by the consul there, his friend William Aldridge. It was the more galling, because some of the sailors had rowed over to the captured ship and found 'ten thousand Dolleres worth of Spaynishe goodes a borde'.

Two days later, they chased another ship. This time, however, there was nothing to take.

The *Hector* sailed on east and in another two days they saw Greece. On 20 April, they anchored off the town of Zante (Zakynthos), capital of the island of the same name, situated a few miles from the north-west coast of the Peloponnese.

Here they were confined to the ship for six days in case they had brought the plague or some other infectious disease from Algiers. Dallam noted the town was a mile long. He couldn't see it clearly, but it had not yet become the elegant place it was by the eighteenth century, with fine architecture, libraries and art collections – a lovely town all but destroyed by the earthquake of 1953. He also knew that the best currants came from Zante, better even than from Corinth, which gave currants their name. I compared the appetite for currants to that for peanuts today. Currants then were consumed in large quantities by everyone – [79]William Lithgow, a Scotsman, said the English were addicted to them. To Zante it was a profitable addiction. Lithgow said that since 1583 the trade had grown to '60,000 chickins' a year. [80]At 9/- a chicken, that is £72,000 a year or, following Bradford, very approximately over seven million a year at today's prices. Like all fashionable foods, currants were soon assumed to cure almost everything. By 1620, 'beside their pleasantness in taste, they excite the appetite, strengthen the stomack, comfort and refresh weak bodies and ... are verrie good and wholesome for evrie season, age and constitution.'

By the end of their quarantine, Dallam had been cooped-up in the *Hector* for well over a month, with one brief excursion into Algiers. During their incarceration at Zante he had looked with longing on a little mountain called Skopos ('Look-out'), some 1,500 foot high and about, he thought, a mile from the town. He imagined how wonderful must the view be from the top. He took a vow that once they were allowed ashore he wouldn't eat or drink or go into the town until he had climbed its verdant slopes and reached the flat top where he thought he could see 'a whyte thinge lyke a rocke'.

He also persuaded Ned Hall the coachman and Michael Watson the joiner to come with him. He paid some sailors to row them to the shore opposite

Skopos and they set off. On their left rose a second small mountain, with a castle called Proveditore, from which the Venetian governor ran the island. (Venice had ruled it since 1485, and it had been a mainstay of their Levant trade. It now paid tribute to the Sultan.)

In fact, they soon realised Skopos was a good deal further than a mile from the shore, but it was very early in the morning, still cool, they were free from the ship and spring was in the air. The birds were singing, the scent of thyme and the flowers for which the island was famous was carried on the light breeze. The Venetians called the island 'Zante – fior de Levant', Flower of the East, because of its glorious flowers.

It was beautiful – but to Michael Watson, frightening. He was clearly an extremely nervous man and had only been persuaded to come by Dallam's much more forceful character. As they mounted, he became more nervous still. They were unarmed, having been ordered to leave all weapons on the ship. All at once they saw above them 'a man goinge with a greate staffe on his shoulder, having a clubbed end, and on his heade a cape which seemed to have five horns standing outryghte'.

This terrifying, almost devilish sight made Watson beg them to turn back. But 'with muche adow' they got him to continue, though Hall was now nearly as nervous. The man, when they reached him, turned out to be a harmless shepherd, with a large herd of sheep and goats. But Watson had had enough and would go no further. Hall muttered 'somethinge fayntly', to the effect he would accompany Dallam to the end.

Not long afterwards, they reached the summit (Hall, too, now begging Dallam to turn back) guided in by a friendly (and unarmed) man who had come to meet them. The top, with its magnificent view across to the sea, was a flat, fair-sized, grassy 'greene' with two lime-white little houses, one of which had a chapel at its end, and a small square house where an anchorite had recently died. Five hundred years old, adds Dallam calmly – and reveals, as he sometimes does, that he lived in a very superstitious age, something no doubt contributing to Watson's and Hall's terrors.[81]

In fact, the people they now met on the mountaintop were extremely friendly. It had grown very hot and they had now walked some four miles from the shore and climbed 1,500 feet. Seeing a man at the far side of the cropped turf pouring water for a second man, Dallam said he was very thirsty and would get some too. Ned Hall hung back, warning him not to go near them, but Dallam 'wente bouldly to the sid of the house' and indicated he would like some water. The man, however, insisted he drank wine and gave him first a bowl of red wine and then, tasting even better in Dallam's view, a bowl of white. He tried to pay him with 'one halfe Dolor of Spanyshe money'. The man refused it, but being offered one of the small, expensive (2/- notes Dallam) pocketknives he had brought from London, hesitated, then took it. At the sight of 'the blad gilded and graven' out of its sheath, he shouted excitedly to a friend, who came running and at once tried to take the knife off him.

Dallam's new companion won this unseemly struggle, and now beckoned him through a cloister into the crowded chapel, sitting him in a pew among the congregation. This was in fact the little Monastery of the Panaghia Skopiotissa, Our Lady of the Look-out, whose ruins can be discerned today. Dallam was fascinated. He had never, he says, seen 'any parte of a Mass before', a rather curious remark which throws ambiguity onto his suspected Catholicism about which I commented earlier. Nor was he used to the women sitting or standing apart, as they did then in Greek Orthodox churches – and still quite often do. In fact, standing up to observe this, he suddenly saw Ned Hall who, having lost Dallam, had crept in and ensconced himself in the middle of the women, causing a good deal of merriment.

The service ended, and as he and Ned Hall started to leave, they were again detained and politely led back through the chapel and into the house outside of which Dallam had been given wine before. Inside were eight women, one very old in black but seven very young and extremely pretty (one notes Dallam becoming increasingly susceptible to attractive women as the voyage progresses). They were sat down and he was given more wine, bread and hard-boiled eggs with rose-coloured shells (Ned would still only drink water). The young women were richly dressed in damask and satin, so Dallam supposed they must live up there; the rose-coloured eggs reminded him of similar ones at country festivals in England. In fact, he had arrived at the monastery at the climax of the Greek Orthodox Easter festivities, for which the girls were dressed. The eggs were Easter eggs. Before long, many more people would arrive from Zante for the final service and the breaking of their Lenten fast.

Dallam and Ned Hale were as intriguing to the Greeks as the Greeks were to them, and the girls gathered round to stare at them, especially when Dallam pressed his last knife (again he emphasises the 2/-) on the old woman. There was much bowing and thanking and, eventually, Dallam and Hale were anxious to find out what had happened to Michael Watson, so they left that enchanted spot.

[82]Magical then, and 'still a magical place,' writes Gerald MacLean, who has seen it recently, 'despite the radio and television towers. The anchorite's tomb has gone, but the view of Zante harbour remains magnificent. The church and outbuildings Dallam visited have been ruined by earthquakes, but a small chapel has been built within the rubble. It is surrounded by wild oats.'

Dallam and Hale found their 'faintharted' friend Michael Watson crouched inside a bush, famished, very thirsty and, when he heard their account, ashamed of his cowardice, so much so that he refused to stay with them when they rejoined the other passengers. 'When our martchantes saw us,' Dallam wrote, they began 'to be verrie angry.' They thought something terrible must have taken place, but 'I bid them howld ther peace' while he described what had actually happened. Both the Greeks present and the merchants were amazed and impressed, and nine of the merchants immediately wanted to go at once and see the Skopos monastery for themselves. Dallam said he was too tired to take them, so they hired a guide and set off.

They returned late that night and thanked Dallam fulsomely for telling them about it. The following two days were spent watching the Greeks at their yearly sports – galloping to pierce a ring with a lance, charging a beam with a sack swinging round when it was hit and similar games. The *Hector* lent them her trumpeters for the day.

Then, on 2 May, they weighed anchor again and sailed away from Zante.

Cyprus – Cats and Snakes

At first, the wind being fair, they went south for 125 miles or so, and then after three days turned east, passing to the north of Cerigo (Kythira), where Dallam was told 'faire Hellin' had been born, and from where she had been seduced and taken to Troy. (In fact, in classical myth, Helen was a Spartan princess and born there.)

By 5 May, the wind had dropped and they sailed slowly along the north coast of Candie, past a place where St Paul had been shipwrecked. Among the highest mountains they passed was one called Crete, which later gave its name to the island, which, at some 300 miles long, is one of the longest in Greek waters.

An old Jew on board told them that on top of that mountain stood a brazen giant to guard the island – an interesting survival in folk memory of an ancient legend. This was of Talus, a bronze giant forged by Hephaestus which he gave Minos to protect Crete. Three times a day he strode round the island and if strangers approached would leap into a furnace and rapidly emerge red hot to burn them up. He was defeated by Medea when she came past Crete with the Argonauts after winning the Golden Fleece. She discovered a secret nail in the giant's foot connected to the single vein coiled through its body. Pulling this plug she let out the fiery fluid that circulated within it, and the giant expired.

They sailed on, clearing the end of Crete and passing the islands of Cassos (Kaisos) and Carpathos (Karpathos) by 7 May. During 8 and 9 May, they were becalmed; then the wind picked up and carried them

Murad III

Above: Ahmed I

Opposite: Mehmed II

A view of the city and castle of Aleppo, Syria, 1754 (engraving), Drummond, Alexander (d.1769)

'Filles de l'Isle de Chio'. Women of Chios

"Femme de l'Isle de Malthe"
NICOLAS DE NICOLAY, Thomas Artus (sieur d'Embry).Date: Paris, Mathieu Guillemot, 1650.

Relics of the Past.

CURIOUS MUSICAL INSTRUMENT OF THE SIXTEENTH CENTURY.

Torments of the Slaves, from Histoire de Barbarie 1637

The Middle Gate of the Topkapi Saray Palace, Istanbul

Topkapi Palace, Istanbul

Topkapi Palace Harem, aerial view, Istanbul

Topkapi Palace, the Harem

Privy Chamber of Sultan Murat III with beds and fireplace in the
Topkapi Palace, Harem, Istanbul

past Paphos on the west coast of Cyprus. By 12 May they had reached Cape Gata.

Here they would have seen from the ship the monastery of St Nicholas of the Cats. The name comes from a terrible war in the Middle Ages between the monks and snakes. These had overrun the Cape and terrorised the inhabitants. Someone suggested cats, so an army of ferocious cats was built up by the monks. These quarrelled fiercely among themselves but were trained to rush forth at the sound of a bell and attack the snakes. Did this really happen? It seems possible. [83]*New Scientist* carried a report fairly recently of how cats were eating the endangered iguanas on the Cayman and Caicos islands in the Caribbean – and iguanas can be just as formidable as snakes. In any event there are neither snakes nor cats in the ruins of the monastery now, but Cape and ruined monastery still keep their names.

At Cape Gata, Parsons showed his usual bloody-mindedness. He put down a Cypriot they had picked up in Zante instead of landing him on Crete, which he'd promised to do. The man had begged for this, something easily done, so as to see his brother whom he'd been trying to get to for several months. Dallam, increasingly irked by Parsons, thought this extremely unfair, which the man also 'thought himselfe, for he wepte bitterly'.

On 12 May they paused but did not land outside Famagusta, which was crowded with shipping, particularly since it was Turkish galleys with their banks of slave-driven oars. Dallam would have seen the huge breaches blasted in the massive city walls when the Turks had finally crushed Venetian resistance a generation before. The Venetian commander, Marcantonio Bragadino, had been skinned alive, his skin stuffed with straw and the grisly trophy sent back to Constantinople.

Dallam thought Cyprus, as they sailed past it, one of the most pleasant and most fruitful places he had ever seen. They didn't stop again but continued under the vicissitudes of the weather, first becalmed, then catching 'a fresh gale of wyndd' and sailing swiftly out south-east from Cyprus, past the mountains of Syria on their port side and finally, on 15 May, anchoring off the place Dallam called Scanderoon (today's Alexandretta/Iskenderun) at the farthest south-eastern corner of the Mediterranean.

Scanderoon

The next day – evidence of how cooped-up they all felt on the *Hector* – Dallam, the engineer John Harvey, Chauncey, the physician, one of the trumpeters and 'Mr Guner' (an important senior figure in charge of all gunnery) along with two of his mates, all set off, rowed to the shore by some sailors, on a hunting expedition. This suggests, incidentally, as did Dallam shopping in Algiers, that to a certain extent the passengers were expected, or allowed, to cater for themselves.

The port of Scanderoon was backed by high mountains – so high that the sun didn't rise above them till ten o'clock and ships had to anchor more than a mile offshore in case they should be trapped by lack of wind.

The few miles of land between the mountains and the sea teemed with game and consisted largely of thick woods with large areas of marsh. The party of seven, equipped with muskets, powder and shot, at times found it almost impenetrable.

They were also apprehensive. Several times they came upon native hunters, lying hidden with bows and arrows or sometimes muskets. They were also apprehensive of wild beasts. After forcing their way for about three miles, they came upon a great 'quagmyer'. Struggling through this, suddenly there were 'tow myghtie greate buffelawes, beasts biger than our greate oxen. At firste we saw nothinge, but there heads, and they made a great noyse with their snufflinge.' Snufflinge gave way to panic and the buffalo sprang up and charged, plunging and splashing, off into the marsh, amazing Dallam that they didn't immediately sink and drown.

But soon afterwards panic seized Dallam and his six companions. They now saw ahead about forty of the native hunters gathered together and, it seemed, trying to encircle them. At once, outnumbered, in an unknown country, terrified, they fled back in the direction of the shore, long out of sight. Torn by brambles, bruised by branches, soaked by patches of bog, they at last broke out of the woods onto a wide plain a mile from the sea and saw, to their relief, the *Hector* riding at anchor on the calm waters. Exhausted and very thirsty, they found a spring of 'verrie comfortable' water to drink and to help them recover.

On the way back to the ship there was yet another extraordinary thing for Dallam to see and record. 'Upon the works of an oulde house, verrie strainge varmint running up and downe at great pace, som of them biger than a great toade, and of the same collore, but they had large tayles lyk a ratt.' The varmints were his first Mediterranean lizards.

The *Hector* was to remain at Scanderoon for nearly a month, and this on a voyage the primary object of which was to bring the Sultan's present from the queen, now years overdue, to Constantinople. The company no doubt felt that having informed Henry Lello, Barton's successor as 'ambassador', that the present was on its way, they could to some extent relax. The one person who did not relax was Lello himself. On the contrary. A highly strung and anxious man to whom we'll come, a newcomer, fighting for his company and his country in an intensely competitive situation, he had to watch while his hated rival, the Frenchman de Brèves, consolidated his power and added to his influence. Without the present, Lello felt hamstrung. Cut off from the Sultan he was, compared to de Brèves, even compared to the Venetians, powerless. He was not even a real ambassador.

[84]But the long stay at Scanderoon was a measure of the importance the Levant Company attached to it. Or rather, not to the port but to Aleppo, some eighty miles inland, to which it was the gateway. Here, enormous caravans would arrive coming up through Persia (Iran) from the Indian Ocean and across from the Red Sea and east Africa – caravans often of between 20,000 and 40,000 camels and mules. The organisation was staggering, yet extremely efficient. They were guarded by cavalry and 400 or so soldiers, and sometimes six pieces of field artillery, each pulled by twelve camels and which terrified raiding Bedouin. Self-sufficient except

for water, so not too dependent on the country through which they passed, they usually moved at night between two o'clock in the morning and sunrise to avoid the ferocious heat, lighting their way by flaring dry-wood torches.

They brought, as well as spices, cloves, pepper and so on from India and the East Indies, more exotic goods – opium, elephants' teeth, squirrel skins and ivory, with slaves, eunuchs and gold from East Africa. This trade brought enormous prosperity, both to the various destinations in Europe, Constantinople and elsewhere, but also to the intermediaries along the way. It could have brought still more. In 1529 the Turks began to dig an early Suez Canal, but eventually gave up. Think if they had continued!

It was, therefore, with Aleppo via Scanderoon that the Levant Company did a great deal of business, and they had much to take on, much to learn and discuss, and much to drop off. The day to start unloading was fixed for 18 May, but early that morning they saw from the ship 'a goodly show of tentes' covering the plain with the spring which had refreshed Dallam and his companions at the end of their abortive hunting expedition. And not only tents. Companies of horsemen, the dreaded Janissaries, according to Dallam, some with 'their neagors to carry their lancis and other weapeins', came galloping down to the shore.

Captain Parsons sent some sailors into the port to investigate and they returned with urgent warnings from the merchants that on no account should they try and land any goods while they could still see tents. It was apparently part of a vast Turkish army from Damascus and they would seize anything they wanted.

The tents continued to appear for the next two weeks, one company leaving at night (like the caravans, they marched when it was dark), while the next one arrived. On 30 May, the French consul came from Aleppo and dined with Captain Parsons and the merchants, among whom would have been John Sanderson, who travelled out on the *Hector*. [85]Unfortunately, his *Travels* doesn't refer to any of this.

His book does, however, refer to the several illnesses he had contracted earlier at Aleppo. Both Aleppo and, even more, Scanderoon were in many ways ghastly places to be stationed. [86]Charles Robson, writing of Scanderoon in 1628, describes the 'gross fogges that both descend from the mountains and ascend from the Moorish (marshy) valleys'. This was compounded by the arrival each year of millions of frogs whose croaking sounded like 'a multitude of jack-calls' and which, as the marshes dried up, died *en masse,* creating a terrible stench of decay. This hell on earth was fiendishly hot in summer, freezing in winter and prone to terrible earthquakes; death was very common, from the miasma of bad air (mal-air, malaria), and other fevers, but also from drink consumed to comfort the desperate Levant Company officers posted there.

[87]In fact, the citadel of Aleppo, such was the ingenuity of the Arabs, was far cooler than it might have been where the air can feel as hot as sixty-five degrees Celsius. It was built on high ground to catch the strongest winds and had tall, hollow 'wind towers' to funnel air down to street level. These were deliberately narrow to provide shade, and also ran at an angle to the sun's trajectory to maximise this. They, too, accelerated the airflow through the city. Dallam doesn't comment on all this. Apart from anything, he didn't even go to Aleppo. He was only at Scanderoon a month, and the terrible heat of a Middle-Eastern summer hadn't yet arrived.

Once the Turkish army had passed, Dallam went into the town quite often, as frequently as he does in Constantinople, his diary shows. And while perfectly aware of social distinctions, he was completely at ease with his 'superiors' as they with him, and if necessary he would stand up to them with considerable briskness.

While chatting in Scanderoon with the merchants one day, pigeons feeding around them, a white pigeon landed among the others. One of the merchants said 'Welcom, Honoste Tom', picked up the pigeon and extracted a message tied to it. It came from Aleppo. The message was dated with the time the pigeon had been released – four hours before. Dallam saw this happen several times.

The little market town of Tarsus was twelve miles east of Scanderoon, and every Friday, market day, the *Hector* sent its longboat to bring fresh provisions. Paul had been born there, and noting that fact – as he has done before with similar reports of the Iron Man on Crete, or the birthplace of Helen, or the plac es where Paul had landed or preached in the past – Dallam shows how alive, vivid and true in his sixteenth-century mind were the legends of the classical past and the events of the Old and New Testaments. Just before they left, he heard that the very spot where Jonah had surfaced after being disgorged by the whale was marked by a rock outside the entrance to the port. At once, the senior 'Mr Guner' and his mate, along with Dallam, John Harvey and two sailors who rowed them out, hurried to see it. They climbed on 'that verrie place' and gathered samphire growing on the rock.

A few days later, on 10 June, the *Hector* weighed anchor and set off, heading north now on the last leg of its long, long journey to Constantinople.

Rhodes

They sailed, in fits and starts with contrary winds, up past the little coastal towns of Asia Minor (Asia the Less to Dallam), whose fortifications he invariably noted, if they had any, until by 27 June, running short of provisions and fresh water, they decided to go ashore at Rhodes, at the far eastern corner of the island. That same day, there took place the first of several deaths on the *Hector* – Thomas Cable, a young man under twenty, son of one of the ship's owners.

Rhodes, where, incidentally, some classical myths had Helen of Troy end her days, had long been an important trading entrepot in the Levant; despite this, both here and in other still relatively remote Greek/Turkish islands where they landed, an English ship was an object of intense – and shameless – curiosity. Dallam records as many as 'five hundrethe Rude Turkes' swarming aboard to stare and poke about, and equal numbers every day they were there.

The Turkish governor of Rhodes was away, but on the 28 June his deputy came aboard with his lieutenants and was entertained in the gunroom, 'one of the Fayereste Romes in the ship'. This seems to have been where Dallam had established himself since he kept his virginals there. His friend, the master gunner, asked him to play them, which Dallam did with great success. As was expected, Parsons gave the deputy a gift of broadcloth, enough to make 'a veste or goune after the Turkie manere'.

The deputy then left, soon followed by Dallam, his friend Harvey, the steward of the ship and some of his men. Their Greek guide led them up into the famously massive walls, which Dallam describes as double-walled with very deep, dry ditches in between. But what really fascinated him were the enormous cannons lying about – 'marvalus greate peesis' – some so large that two men could fit down the barrel side by side and which, the guide told them, took two hours to reload after each discharge. Some had been fired so often they had burst. These were all relics of the last great battle there seventy-seven years before, the siege of 1522. Six hundred Knights of St John and six thousand men-at-war had withstood one hundred thousand Turks for five months. So courageous had they been that the Turks had allowed them the honours of war and let them leave freely, first for Crete, then for Malta.

The little group, relieved, as Dallam notes, to have circled the town unmolested, returned to the entrance gate, paused long enough to drink 'a pitcher of wyne which coste us but one penye' and set off back to the ship. They were soon waylaid by Mr May.

May, 'our preatcher', had a reputation for causing difficulties and chaos. Sanderson describes him as 'troblesom May' and 'that factiouse man and peevish humorest' who would play irritating practical jokes. This had already irritated the merchants at Aleppo, where he had been chaplain, and the Levant Company had therefore recalled him. May had ignored this and was going to Constantinople, where there was already a chaplain, hoping the company would accept having, and paying for, another. This was not entirely a vain hope because Henry Lello, temperamentally gloomy, was known to be intensely religious and was anxious to have an Anglican church in the city to stand against the sea of heathen and heretical religions.

May was about to cause more trouble. Wanting to see a little inside the town himself, he asked Dallam and his companions to come back with him, promising to look inside and at once leave. They did so, whereupon May, having spotted some fountains running with fresh water, persuaded them to go a little further inside. Again they did so. Two Turks came up and said to May, 'Parlyi Francko, sinyore?'[88] May, who spoke a little Italian, said he did. Whilst he and a companion chatted to them, Dallam was beckoned over to his stall by a Turk who had heard him play his virginals and was so delighted he had 'kissed me aborde our ship'. He made clear they were all in danger and should leave at once, which Dallam and his friends did 'as faste as theye could'.

Looking back as they ran, they were surprised, and rather alarmed, to see that Mr May, lingering on to show off his Italian, and his companion, had vanished.

Back on board, Dallam had his first serious altercation with Captain Parsons. He went to the captain and described what had happened. This autocratic, strong-willed man was evidently becoming increasingly exasperated by Dallam 's cocksureness, popularity and central position to the voyage, despite being only a humble craftsman, and because he himself had already had to rely on him for his own safety. Captain Parsons seems to have rapidly lost his temper. Dallam must have known perfectly well that it was dangerous for Christians to explore the town. He and his companions had clearly caused deep offence. It was 'our faulte these men weare taken prisoners'. Dallam, in his diary, now uses a formula he was to resort to on several similar occasions: 'What words did pass betwixt our Mr and me I will omit till God send us into England.'

An odd formula. Beyond making clear, as he has several times, that he intends to write up and extend his diary on his return – which he may well have done, in which case it has vanished – one wonders why he always concealed any details of his clashes with authority. It is possible that he was nervous his diary might be found and read – a risk all diarists take. Yet there were already things he left in, like his account of Parsons' unfairness over booty, which the captain, at least, would have disliked. But I can't think of a more likely reason.

The next morning a letter arrived from Mr May '[w]rytten so pitifully as yf they were presoneres thar seven years'. He described how they had been roughly seized, bound with chains of cold, rusty iron 'as they had been tow Dogges' and confined to a deep, dank dungeon, with whips shaken over them and subject to terrible threats – even 'that they myghte be presently put to Deathe'.

Shocked and alarmed, Parsons and five senior merchants decided, with some courage, to re-enter the town alone and try and rescue May, '[t]roblesom' perhaps, but now, it seemed, in a country where arbitrary execution of enemies and infidels was perfectly common, in real trouble.

The deputy governor made them wait. At last he consented to hear the deputation. One of the men, who spoke Italian, asked 'how they Durste be so bould as to make stay of any of our men, we beinge goinge with so Riche a presente to the Grand Sinyor'. Making use of Dallam even in his absence, they pretended one of the men imprisoned with May (and May a Divine!) was in fact 'the chefe and principall man for the presente'. Unless they were all released at once, the captain would hire a galley and race to inform the Sultan as rapidly as possible of the way they were treated.

It now became clear what was wrong. Parsons had not given a present to the governor. When it was pointed out that, on the contrary, he had given enough cloth to make a handsome 'veste' for the governor, the deputy governor said that in that case he himself had not been given a present. If that were forthcoming, May would be released. 'Heare,' notes Dallam, 'you maye see the base and covetous condition of these Rude and barbarous doged Turkes, and how little they do regard Christians.'

What everyone could also see, since it is clear from Dallam's report that everything that happened was immediately gossiped about all over the ship, was that Parsons' earlier attack on, particularly, Dallam for causing May's arrest had nothing to do with it. Irritating for the captain.

And so the incident, dangerous for a while, was resolved. They had already restocked the ship with provisions and fresh water, and suddenly we sense in Dallam's prose the exhilaration of his extraordinary voyage; 'next day beinge the 30th, or last day of June we wayed ankor, hoysed saile, and so to sea'.

Samos

The exhilaration, as they sped away, did not last very long owing, as always, to the vicissitudes of the wind. At first Dallam was amazed by the multitude of little Aegean islands they were threading. At one point, standing on the deck, he said he could see 'no less than 16 islandes' round them (difficult from the map to see where he could have been), but as they neared Samos the wind changed and they had to anchor in front of a small town and wait for it to change again. They were to be trapped round Samos until 11 July.

The inhabitants were clearly terrified at their arrival – evidence of the prevalence of invading piracy – and everyone watched as the people rushed about the fields driving cattle into the mountains and emptying a small ship they had hauled ashore – 'but they touke more paynes than theie needed, for we ment them no harme'. Several times they tried to continue but each time were forced back by the wind. On 8 July came the second death aboard, 'one John Knill', a servant of one of the ship's owners who was sailing on it.

It was on Samos that Pythagoras had proved, on a massive scale, his theorem about the right-angled triangle. You can see near Pythagoria the tunnel bored under a small mountain by which he did this. Samos is a large island, the east coast very close to the Asia Minor mainland, and on 10 July they tried again to sail round its western end; again they were beaten back as far as the little town from which they had started. It was dark when they arrived and they decided to go into it and get provisions and water, both running low. But 'by the necklyience of him that sounded they ran aground'. This 'turned us to greate feare', and they struggled to refloat the ship all night – probably by 'warping' in which the anchor is carried out by a small boat, dropped into the sea and then by winching it on board the ship is slowly dragged free.[89]

The morning saw the menacing arrival of four galleys and a frigate, clearly planning to trap and board the *Hector*, and this caused Captain Parsons to set off at once, not by the west coast, but by the much more difficult but much closer east coast. The strait was only just over half a mile wide, and the galleys came up close on their starboard or right side. As they come closer and closer, Parsons had the whole company line the decks and opened the gun ports and, as the galley came alongside, the trumpeters suddenly blasted off – 'So we Dashte them oute of Countinance who mente to have feared us.'

The *Hector* had escaped, and escape was now urgent. This is the only time in the whole voyage that Dallam mentions his diet. The ship, as far as he was concerned at least, was down to rice boiled 'in stinking water, and our beveredge did also stinke'.

Two days later, speeding across the wine-dark Aegean, they sighted Chios, and on the evening of 14 July the ship anchored a mile or two off the coast. Early next morning, now desperate for food and water, the longboat went ashore.

Chios and Its Seductive Women

Before the boat set off, several of the 'jentlemen passengers' asked Dallam if he would come ashore with them for, as they said, 'theye did know he would not leave me behinde'. They were scarcely in the boat when 'he' appeared leaning over *Hector*'s side and yelled down that Dallam must come back into the ship *at once*; 'but the jentlemen had me betwyxte them, and helde me faste, nether did I meane to dow as he bid me.' Seeing he could do nothing, Parsons warned them that if they took so much as a bunch of grapes they would be imprisoned on the spot for at least a year. He also said that if Dallam wasn't on the longboat when it returned, the *Hector* would sail at once.

Ignoring him, the party set off towards land, heading for a little town, possibly Kaltimasia, visible a mile or so inland.

[90]The large island of Chios is one of the most fertile, most beautiful and most interesting of the Aegean islands, known then as The Great Turk's Aegean Garden. It is famous for its mastic plant – *Pistacia lentiscus*. This evergreen shrub, which has a gnarled, crooked stem and can reach six feet tall, can be found all along the Mediterranean but is only cultivated extensively by twenty-two villages – the Mastichachoria – in the south of Chios. It is mentioned in the Old Testament, the *bakha* of Psalm [84]. *Bakha* is derived from the Hebrew word for crying or weeping, and mastic shrubs not only secrete 'tears' of resin when cut but their branches sound like someone weeping when broken and walked on. The resin is collected in metal cups from the sliced stems. Before modern dentistry, the whole world suffered from bad breath, and mastic gum, with its fairly pleasant medicinal flavour, was used by the Romans and thereafter to combat this. And it was especially sought by the Ottoman sultans for themselves and their harems. When Dallam arrived, the twenty-two mastic villages were owned by the Sultana. Today it is still used in chewing gum, as a flavouring in food, drinks and ice cream, and medicinally to soothe stomachs.

Almost as soon as they had landed, they were, as always, the centre of the amazed curiosity of many of the townspeople, who, since it was Sunday, were promenading by the shore. These gathered to stare at them, and the numbers increased when they actually entered the town. They were at once directed to the consul. This friendly figure welcomed them and invited them up some ladder-like stairs on to a platform erected from the back of his house from where they could see their ship riding at anchor. Six 'verrie beauteful' women who were sitting with him politely left when they arrived. The consul had 'a verrie fine bankette' of sweetmeats and cakes set before them, served with a raspberry drink. He also sent some of his men to buy provisions for them.

Unfortunately, their presence soon caused the consul a good deal of trouble. The inhabitants were now so curious that, despite him shouting at them and waving them away, they began to clamber up on to the dry stone wall at the end of his garden in such numbers that it eventually collapsed. Seeing how 'troublsom' they were becoming, Dallam and his companions decided to leave. The consul's men had now returned almost empty handed. Since it was Sunday, all they could get was a bushel of garlic – not much but certainly better than nothing and gratefully accepted and paid for.

As they came down the ladder-stairs, they saw in the distance the longboat returning to the *Hector* – signal for their ship to depart.

But they were temporarily distracted by a pleasant surprise awaiting them as they came into the street, a surprise which, incidentally, suggests ships didn't just land on Chios for fresh supplies or for mastic. Lined up were 'the chefeste women in town'. Their breasts were naked, their complexion amazingly fresh and clear, they were richly dressed and, writes Dallam, he thought they were the most beautiful women in the world.

The women of Chios were famous for their beauty and, something Dallam evidently didn't know, not just for their beauty but for their love-making and the pleasure and freedom with which they exercised their skills. [91]Mayes quotes William Lithgow writing a few years later: 'The women of the Citty of Sio [Chios] are the most beautiful Dames ... of all Greekes, upon the face of the earth, and greatly given to venary ... Their husbands are their Pandors and when they see any strangers arrive, they will presently demand of him; if he have a Mistresse: and so they make Whoores of their owne Wives ... If a Straunger be desirous to stay all night with any of them, their price is a Chicken [zecchini] of gold, nine shillings English, out of which this companion receiveth his supper, and for his paines, a belly full of sinfull content.'

That their breasts were naked is an interesting echo of Minoan and Mycenaean wall paintings. Perhaps Helen had naked breasts on appropriate occasions, and the practice may have once been common all over the Aegean and mainland Greece.

On the other hand, there may be a less lively but more accurate explanation for the naked breasts of Chios. Gerald MacLean in his typically interesting and informative essay on William Biddulph's *Travels* (1600–12) notes that the first French edition of Nicolay's *Navigations* (1568) reports that naked breasts was a way of recognising prostitutes on Malta and various other Mediterranean islands (see illustration page 00).

Dallam and his jentlemen companions soon regained their ship, which, as they had known perfectly well, hadn't moved an inch. They were pleased to find that their garlic, which they kept and ate, could have easily been sold to other passengers at a profit.

The wind was fair, and the same day 'Ankor was wayed, and we under sail'.

Deaths at Sea

The next stage of the voyage, from 16 July to 5 August, was bedevilled by contrary winds, or no wind, and by a powerful current against them coming down from the Hellespont.

They were becalmed for two days before the town of Chios a little way up the island. Here Parsons, who had earlier said the consul there, Mr Armitage, was a friend of his, refused to let anyone land, fearful he might have to dispense more presents.

On 19 July they came to the island of Tenedos. Dallam thinks it is opposite the site of Troy on the mainland, but in fact it was opposite Alexandria Troas, in Hellenistic and Roman times the main port of north-west Asia Minor. Troy itself still lay buried under the grassy hillock of Hissarlik at the northern end of the plain, waiting to be discovered by Schliemann in 1871. But travellers in the seventeenth and eighteenth centuries often explored the fallen walls and broken columns of ruined Troas thinking, like Dallam and the rest of those on the *Hector*, that it was Homer's Troy. The ruins did, however, have some historical significance. It was here that Paul had his vision of the Macedonian who said 'Come and help us', and it was from Troas he set out on his mission to the West.

The *Hector* was held up again by contrary winds until 21 July, and that day there was a third death, 'a boye called John Felton, who was borne at Yarmouthe'.

[92]It is worth a brief digression here to comment on the *Hector*'s three deaths so far. Death at sea was very common. Three in five months was good going. Drake, who was himself eventually to die of dysentery, lost more than twice that number a month into his expedition of 1572, setting off with a crew of 164 and returning with only fifty-seven. The main cause was not drowning or battles at sea but disease. Precisely, dysentery – 'the bloody flux' – ship's fever or typhus, scurvy and, though rarely, plague.

The rapid inflation all over Europe towards the end of the sixteenth century, which led to an equally rapid increase in shipboard disease generally, may paradoxically have saved the *Hector*. In England, as elsewhere, the price of victuals rose very quickly: beer and beef, for instance, up fifty per cent during the 1580s. Contractors, anxious to retain the supplying of cost-conscious ship owners like the Levant Company, salted only the cheapest cuts of beef and threw in offal, bone and hoof; meat was already going bad when it was salted into the cask. So, the beer went sour, the biscuits mouldy and worm-eaten, the beef and cheese rotten, and as a result food poisoning and dysentery spread. Water taken from the bilges or in buckets from harbours was often awash with sewage or rubbish. Rats became bold through starvation, but at least they could be eaten.

The *Hector* was saved from all this probably because she carried Levant Company merchants, owners of the ship and other important passengers. These, as we've noted, to an extent relied on their own purchases to augment their diet. Parsons seems, as a result of such passengers, to have decided, given his meanness, or been instructed, not to lay in either substandard or very expensive food, but to rely on regular stops to take on fresh supplies. This in turn meant that no one on board had scurvy, an appalling disease where limbs swelled up and turned black, healed fractures cracked, teeth fell out in mouthfuls and blood trickled continually from nostrils and eyes.

In fact, long before the eighteenth century when the cause – lack of fresh fruit and vegetables, i.e. vitamin C – was established, some English captains knew the cure already. Hawkins' son Richard wrote that 'most fruitful for this sickness is raw oranges and lemons ... a certain remedy'.

On the *Hector*, a fairly continuous flow of fresh fruit and vegetables provided the same prophylactic. Nevertheless, this third death made some of them anxious.

The same day that Felton died, some Turkish galleys came towards them from the Hellespont. Now in an increasing panic that he might, as expected, have to disburse present after present, Parsons quickly up-anchored and set sail. The wind dropped and he had to anchor again, only to pull it up for the same reason when two Turkish frigates appeared. Stopped from boarding by the *Hector* moving, one came alongside and two Englishmen shouted up that a Turkish admiral would soon be arriving with more galleys. Parsons would be able to identify the admiral's ship because he 'had tow lanthornes on his poupe and the Reste but one a peece'.

The galleys came gliding majestically into view shortly afterwards; a marvellous sight, wrote Dallam, great banks of oars rhythmically swinging together plied by naked slaves, the galleys brightly painted, the sails, which galleys used as well as oars in a fair wind, billowing white or deep blue.

Parsons was not, however, to escape scot-free. As the galleys drew level, he fired a three cannon salute – 'meserably done,' said Dallam, echoing the critical comments of the sailors. It produced an instant and outraged response. A boat at once came across with the captain of the nearest galley. Why such an insulting acknowledgement for an admiral? In any case, where was the admiral's present? Parsons replied he'd no idea there *was* an admiral. Had he known, every gun on his ship would have fired. As for a present, he was now forced to disgorge two small chests of expensive Holland linen. The captain of the galley now asked where was *his* present? Parsons said he hadn't got anything. Eventually, the Turk accepted some tobacco and a pipe.

The *Hector* continued on under a weak wind, but was forced to anchor again a little further north opposite the point where the fortress town of Sigeum once stood. Here Dallam and his friend Harvey went ashore with a hammer, with which, like a tourist today, he knocked a chunk off a marble pillar; he thought the ruins there were still part of Troy.

And so, on 22 July, the ship entered the Hellespont, that sixty-five-kilometre long sea passage we now call the Dardanelles. The wind was continually capricious and for over a week, often becalmed, they slowly made their way up towards Constantinople. But slowly not just because of the wind. The Black Sea is higher than the Mediterranean and a strong current flows down from it to the Aegean, making Byron's feat of swimming acroos it on 3 May 1810 all the more splendid. [93](Sanderson, who was on the voyage, says the ship ran aground at the entrance to the Dardanelles, resulting 'in some danger'. His account of the trip, though it corroborates Dallam, is very short. Dallam doesn't think the incident worth mentioning.)

By the beginning of August, it was five and a half months since they had left London. This was not bad going for so long a journey and they had now penetrated deep into the Turkish Empire. Their goal was less than 250 miles ahead, but one group – or rather one man – was desperate they should reach it as fast as possible.

The man was Henry Lello, the would-be, should-be but still not the accredited English ambassador in Constantinople. The degree of his desperation, still being humiliated by both the French and the Venetian ambassadors, can be gauged by the fact that he had just dispatched a very fast boat to pick up and carry back, as well as any diplomatic bags, the most important men on the *Hector*.

At Last – Constantinople!

The most important men from Lello's agitated point of view were the men who would work on the Sultan's present and on the present for the queen mother.

These were Dallam himself, his engineer John Harvey, his joiner Richard Watson, his painter Rowland Buckett, and Ned Hall the coachman for the queen mother's coach; also in the party to Constantinople were Mr May the preacher, a new cook and underbutler for Henry Lello, Mr Bailey (eventually to cause considerable chaos), a Mr Gonzale (renowned for his strength), Mr Sharpe, Mr Lambert, a Janissary sent to guard them, and two others. The leader of the group was Thomas Glover. They all left with an alacrity spurred by the physicians on board who were worried that one of the sailors might have the plague; it was a false alarm, probably prompted by the latest death. In all, there were sixteen in the party.

Dallam describes Lello's boat as 'chiurmagee' from 'chiurme' or slaves who rowed it. It also had sails, so in effect a little galley. The boat could carry only six passengers, so Glover hired two more similar boats.

[94]It is worth looking briefly at Thomas Glover, an important figure in the Levant Company and, behind the scenes, in the events now unfolding. With an English father and Polish mother from Dantzig, he was born at sea on the way back to England from Poland, but he was brought up in Constantinople. He spoke fluent Polish, English, Italian and Turkish, and he was particularly at home among the Ottomans of Constantinople. He had, like Lello, been on the embassy staff under Barton and had already made a fortune in the Levant. (Though not strictly meant to, all the top Levant Company figures traded on their own behalf and made very large sums of money. Lello was to do so, as did Sanderson, Paul Pindar, and the rest of them). Glover was sailing out now to become secretary to Lello, whom he would eventually succeed. He was decisive and cool in an emergency, proud, hot-tempered and had a violent streak. It was not unknown then to hit servants, but Glover seems to have been excessive. When the master of his household, George Coxden, was reported speaking ill of him, Glover had him beaten on his bare feet – 'bastinadoed' – a particularly barbarous punishment. Glover joined in the beating. It seems he did this sort of thing with more than one servant.

But from Dallam's point of view what was most noticeable and valuable was that Glover was an extremely experienced traveller, who knew Turkey very well indeed. He knew, and Dallam commented on it, that the sort of penny-pinching measures practised by Parsons were completely counter-productive. He also led the party with an attractive *panache*. Forced, on 7 August, to land at midnight because there was no wind, and the rowers were exhausted, Glover had them build an enormous bonfire out of an old hedge against the walls of a ruined castle they found and roast a sheep he'd bought the day before when they'd paused briefly at Gallipoli.

They left the castle before dawn, but now the wind became so strong they had to land again at Marmara Ereglisi a little further up the coast. Here, as before, Glover's knowledge of how to travel impressed Dallam. Some of the party invaded a vineyard and stole some grapes. The Greek owners were naturally furious but, beaten off by the hugely powerful Mr Gonzale, could only complain to the governor. By an embarrassing chance, this friendly man was actually with them, delivering a present of another sheep. Mr Glover was immediately, wrote Dallam, 'verrie willing to make the Greekes restitution for the hurte that was done them'. And having 'made us all frendes', he cemented the goodwill by giving the governor, when they left, '2 or 3 peecis of goold caled chickenes'.

The sea was now so rough and the wind so high they were forced to tow the boats while they tramped ten miles along the shore to Chora, something in the circumstances both difficult and dangerous. From here they walked to Ganos, a large village set in very wild, wooded country some way back from a low cliff from which they could see the sea. Glover seems to have been suspicious of the very poor inhabitants and found a little house for them to sleep in outside the village.

The night that followed was wild and, for a while, terrifying – until it descended into farce; which, in retrospect, gave Dallam a good deal of pleasure.

In retrospect – but not immediately. The house was perched on the edge of a low cliff. A ladder led up to a balcony, which in turn had a little door which led into a room where they would have to sleep, Dallam writes gloomily, on bare boards. This is the only time on the voyage that he mentions what must have been quite frequent discomforts. On this whole short trip up the Dardanelles, lasting about three weeks, they could never get out of their clothes, he says, never change them, never wash properly, nor sleep in a bed. But this particular night clearly marked a climax in discomfort. There was nothing in the room, he still gloomily continues, except a shelf with two pitchers and some earthenware plates. There wasn't even a window – just a small hole in the stone wall.

It was soon after they had moved in, and after eating, that some of them set off down towards the sea through the 'wildernesses and deserte wood'. Lizards and various unrecognisable 'varmiin' scuttled away from them. Remembering 'what hard lodginge' they would have, they gathered armfuls of bracken and 'softe weed' to lie on and have as pillows.

It grew dark. They chose where they would each sleep and laid out the heaps of soft weed. The Janissary accompanying them stretched out on a loose board covering the gap down to the stable some way below. They were clearly all apprehensive about the people of the village, because they decided to sleep with their drawn swords beside them. Two of them had 'musketes'. But only half an hour after they had lain down they were attacked – 'tormented' – by a whole host of biting, creeping, itching creatures 'which did bite farr worss than fleaes' and which had swarmed out of their improvised bedding. Leaping up, they threw it out into the night and roughly swept the room but couldn't, said Dallam, no doubt having not washed for days and itching a good deal already, 'clense our selves so downe'.

They subsided onto the bare boards again. A strong wind had got up and as it moaned round the house, Glover, his memory stimulated by the disturbances, described in vivid detail the things he'd seen in his travels there, the poisonous adders, dangerous 'sarpentes', snakes and other strange 'varmen and beastes'. A few of them slept. Dallam clearly couldn't, but lay in the darkness, listening to the wind and the distant sea.

Around midnight, Mr Bailey got up to go and have a pee. One of his long silk garters, which he'd loosened when he lay down, trailed after him as he stepped carefully over his companions to the little door leading to the balcony outside. No sooner was he through it than the wind, now blowing with gale force, slammed it behind him and at the same time whipped his garter round both legs so that he could hardly move. Mr Bailey, his mind still full of Glover's stories, now thought he had been attacked by snakes. He tried to get back through the door but, unable to find it, fettered by snakes, suddenly panicked and yelled out again and again 'Serpents! Serpents! Serpents!'

At once pandemonium broke out. Hearing Bailey shouting above the wind, everyone inside panicked too. They thought they were being attacked, not by snakes but by murderous villagers, some of whom, as they all leapt up and grabbed their swords, seemed to be in the pitch dark room already. One man, flailing about with his sword, brought the shelf crashing down with all the earthenware on it. Another, who couldn't find his sword, tried to escape up the chimney and brought much of that down too. The Janissary, hired to guard them, terrified by the shouting, shoved aside the plank and dropped down into the darkness of the stable below.

It took Glover to calm things down. Mr Bailey finally found the door from the balcony and staggered in out of the night. At first he was too breathless to speak, but eventually gasped out that a serpent had attacked him. At once Glover realised nothing serious was wrong and, finding Mr Bailey's garter still blowing in the wind, located the 'snake'. Once order was restored, he called a roll. Only the Janissary was missing, until faint cries came from under the floor. The Turk was unable to get out, but, just able to reach his fingers, Mr Gonzale, with his immense strength, was able to haul him up with one hand.

It was fortunate no one was badly hurt, though the man who had pulled the chimney down on his head had a painful wound. However, it had all been enough for Mr Sharpe and Mr Lambert and two of the other men in the party. They decided to make the rest of the trip by land – a three-day journey.

The next day the rest of the party rejoined their boats and continued east. Nothing of any consequence happened on this last leg, except they saw a line of twenty-four windmills on a hill near Heraclia. A day later they were sailing up the Marmara and on Wednesday 15 August, they finally arrived in the Bosphorus and Constantinople. (The *Hector* arrived the next day so, despite Lello's agitation, they had gained no time.)

The voyage had taken six months and three days and they had come, according to a note Dallam made at the start of his diary, 1,090 leagues. With a league a variable distance, but usually 3.456 statute miles (and still being used in England in the nineteenth century), 1,090 leagues makes 3,767.04 miles. But Dallam seems to have been told that before he set out, since he leaves out the whole stretch from Scanderoon, up through the Aegean, the Dardanelles and the Marmara to the Bosphorus and Constantinople. My own rough calculation makes the entire journey just over 5,000 miles. Six months was good going.

But the most testing, important and sometimes frightening time, as far as Dallam was concerned, lay ahead. He, his organ and Henry Lello were all about to engage with the much feared – and justly so – Ottoman Sultan, Mehmed III.

CHAPTER 4

Dallam, the Ottomans and Constantinople in 1599

Disaster

Before dropping anchor, the *Hector* seems to have paused first at the Seven Towers, or *Yedikule* in Turkish, to be joined by Dallam and his party. *Yedikule* is physically attached to the inside of the old Theodosian city walls, having been added five or so years after the conquest of 1453. Originally intended to be a fortress, it was, in fact, never actually used as one. Instead it was partly used by the Imperial Treasury and partly as a prison with a truly terrible reputation. It was called The Seven Towers as as when finished that is what it had, four of them part of the old city walls and three added by the Turks, although only four remain today. It is where tanners – probably by force – were made to congregate.

Tanning was an extremely disgusting business then, involving human urine and much scraping of dead flesh which had been allowed to putrify over several months. All this was to 'un-hair' the skins. Later, dog faeces or animal brains were pounded in to 'purify' the leather.

Today, chemicals, machinery and tannin have made the process relatively smell-free, but in the past the combination of urine, animal faeces and decaying flesh on a vast scale, (eventually there were 300 tanners crowded there), made an appalling stench. No one of quality, said Evliya Çelebi writing at the time, could possibly live there. The tanners, on the other hand, perfectly used to the smell, were equally disgusted by the smell of some 'musk-perfumed dandy'.[95]

In its day, the citadel was more feared than the Bastille or the Tower of London – ambassadors were imprisoned there and the Sultan's enemies executed. [96]Mansel describes how it had its first distinguished victims on 1 November 1463. David Comnenus, last Greek Emperor of Trebizond on the Black Sea, believed to be corresponding with the Sultan's enemies, was murdered – along with his six sons, a brother and a nephew – in front of his wife the Empress Helena. Their bodies were flung to the local dogs and devoured. The empress was fined for trying to bury them. Today, this once fearsome place hosts pop concerts.

After the Seven Towers, the ship swept on, and by 16 August, 1599 had anchored offshore opposite what Dallam calls 'the Surralia' – i.e. the seraglio or harem. In fact, most foreigners referred to the vast Topkapi Palace by this single aspect of it – a prurience in the eyes of many future commentators, who prefer to describe the harem (not entirely accurately, as we'll see) in terms of a convent.

And as the *Hector* sailed in, Dallam would have seen the magnificent panorama spreading around him about which Aaron Hill, a visitor in 1700, wrote, 'For my part, when I was there for the first time, methought I was entering an Inchanted Island.'[97]

Constantinople, even more than other great cities of water – Venice, say, or London or Amsterdam – is dominated by the sea that embraces it on three sides: behind the *Hector*, the Sea of Marmara, up which she had just sailed and which narrowed behind her into the Dardanelles and so back again to the Aegean; ahead, the Bosphorus, also narrowing and finally reaching the Black Sea; and to the left, as it were, the north-west, the growing city was split by a broad ribbon of the Bosphorus six kilometres long and one wide – the Golden Horn. This was so named because it turned gold in the setting sun, but in the blazing August of Constantinople's continental summer it would have sparkled during the day for Dallam.

To the ship's left, or west, rose what was still the main city – the old Byzantine capital. Dallam would have seen part of the great walls and made out the outlines of the Topkapi Palace, and beyond it the domes and minarets of the mosque of Hagia Sophia, and beyond and around that the mosques of Mehmed II, The Conqueror, of Bayezid II, Selim I and of Suleyman the Magnificent. Over to the east, across two or three miles of the Bosphorus, was the Asian part of the city, now Üsküdar, a confused conglomeration of villages, mosques and palaces.

The very next day, 17 August, Captain Parsons, very aware of the crucial role his ship was to play in the carefully choreographed stages to impress the Sultan and the Ottomans, ordered the whole of the *Hector* to be repainted.

Even more crucial here, of course, were the two presents, the coach and the organ, especially the organ. [98]On that same day, the crates containing it were off-loaded onto a lighter and taken across the Golden Horn towards Galata. There was no bridge then and Dallam could well have been reminded of the Thames by the mass of barges, lighters, kayaks and little boats carrying people, goods, messages and troops plying to and fro from shore to shore, serving in effect to unite the divided city. Fifteen thousand people serviced and created this incessant movement. In a view drawn in ink by Melchior Lorck in 1559, sails and masts almost hide the glittering water.

Galata itself, even in Byzantine times, had had autonomy under Genoa, and most of its privileges continued for three centuries after the conquest in 1453, though it had to pay taxes to the Sultan.

In 1477, in a census of households in both Constantinople and Galata done for the Sultan, the proportion of Muslim households to non-Muslim was fifty-nine per cent Muslim to forty-one per cent non-Muslim, and Galata especially showed how in that (fairly) tolerant country all religions could live peacefully together. By 1600, the population in Galata had shifted in favour of foreigners.

It was still Italian in feel, and had become what one could call the centre of the ex-pat community: the traders, merchants and diplomats who lived in Constantinople were Greek, English, French, Armenians, Venetians, Italians ... It was an island of Christians (and of the Jews who'd fled from Spain) in an Islamic sea. Like ex-pat communities the world over, a good number of the inhabitants were shamed by a culpable lack of interest or curiosity in their temporary foreign home and never even bothered to cross the Golden Horn and see the great city opposite them. In Galata they could wear their national costume (across the Horn it was still advisable to dress Turkish, though by the time Dallam was there this seems to have been becoming less necessary). 'They permit all Christians,' wrote Richard Staper, 'both Greeks and Latins, to live their religion and freely use their conscience.'99

And live not just their religion. Galata was the most free and most pleasure-loving part of Constantinople (and thereby, incidentally, the most inappropriate posting for someone with the puritan temperament of Henry Lello). Every Lent there was an uninhibited carnival. 'One would think one was in a town in Italy,' wrote Marcantonio Pignafetta, and a Turkish writer of the seventeenth century said, 'Who says Galata says taverns – may God forgive us!' Taste was refined – in summer the beer was iced with snow carried down from the mountains above Bursa – and the women were so beautiful and so seductively dressed they could *de fare di un sainte un diavole* – turn a saint into a devil.

This process was no doubt facilitated by those taverns, not always so refined and often doubling as brothels. 100Çelebi, 'famous for his love of exaggeration', as Mather puts it, said there were 200 taverns and wine booths serving not just wine or beer but *arak*, a very powerful fermentation of rice and sugar. If a Janissary was caught drinking there – a considerable temptation – he was sewn into a sack and thrown into the fast-flowing Bosphorus, an ancient form of execution used by the Romans to punish those who stole state secrets and which the Ottomans regarded as perfectly civilised – a reasonable conclusion when we compare their practices in this area with ours during this time. For instance, when a Jewish woman was torn to pieces by Janissaries who had accused her of debasing the coinage in which they were paid, Sultana Safiye, the valide of Sultan Mehmed III, was deeply shocked. 'If it was determined that the Jewish woman had to be punished by death,' she said, 'why did it have to be in such an obscene fashion? Why couldn't she just have been thrown into the sea?'[101]

Galata had become a second, if rather smaller, city. The name was derived from 'gala', the Greek for 'milk', because it was where in Byzantine times herdsmen lived with their herds. [102]Pallis makes the name a survival from the Galatians who once had a settlement there, which seems more likely.

The Levant Company had two properties. The first, on the waterfront, was for the merchants and factors and was not comfortable. [103]In 1600, Sanderson wrote peevishly to Nicholas Salter of the Levant Company that it leaked badly, 'it raynes in every rome ... it must be all tiled over'. [104]His habitual bad temper can't have been improved by the fact that he made himself so unpopular by his methods of extracting a special levy called 'a loan' – partly to pay for the organ – that a body of merchants stormed into his room and while one held him fast another hit him repeatedly in the face with a stone. They then stormed out, leaving him to vent his fury on his apprentice, who hated him and had watched his beating-up grinning. He was still seething some weeks later when he wrote to his friend Nicholas Leate in London, describing 'the madmen ... monsters, beasts, whoremongers' with whom he was dealing.[105]

The crates carrying the organ would have been unloaded here and normally the practice was for a Janissary to come to the lighter, collect the tax of three to five per cent and give a receipt. But the organ, as an important present, would not have attracted tax and the crates would have been lugged up the hill through the Galata streets, narrow like nearly all the streets in Constantinople but not nearly so chaotic, crowded but straighter, and the red-tiled wooden houses painted in pleasing pastel shades.

At the top, they reached the heights of Pera, clothed in vines and noted for its pure air (Pera is Greek for 'beyond' – beyond the Golden Horn). Here were the large houses of the rich merchants and the ambassadors, each with fine gardens. The vines, the gardens, the beauty of Galata has now been almost entirely obliterated by urban sprawl, deafening traffic, high-rise apartments, offices, hotels, hostels. All that remains is the Galata tower – sixty-one metres high, with a diameter of nearly nine metres and walls 3.75 metres thick and still magnificent, though Mehmed II, The Conqueror, ordered it to be reduced by seven metres to make it a less visible sign of the people he'd conquered. It is still said in guidebooks 'that in the 17th century Ahmed Çelebi flew a hang glider the 3,000 yards across the Bosphorus to the Asian part of the city, Üsküdar'. In 1997 the Turkish director Mustapha Altioklar made a successful film about it called *Istanbul Beneath My Wings*. Alas, the story was a myth.[106]

[107]However, the myth may not be entirely without foundation. In his book, *Dark Side of the Moon*, Gerard J DeGroot, Professor of Modern History at St Andrew's University in Scotland, describes how the first gunpowder rocket was launched on the banks of the Bosphorus in 1623. Ahmed (whom Groot calls Hasan) Çelebi, to impress the Sultan Murad IV and celebrate the birth of his daughter, packed twenty-five kilograms of gunpowder below a conical wire cage. Then he said to the Sultan, 'Your majesty, I leave this world to talk with the prophet Jesus. Your majesty, Jesus sends his greetings!' Then he climbed into the cage, a friend lit the fuse and moments later a colossal explosion hurled Çelebi nearly 1,000 feet into the air above the Bosphorus. At his apogee, he sprang out, opened some home-made wings and drifted safely back to earth. The watching crowds cheered wildly and the Sultan gave him a purse of gold and a commission in the cavalry.

The crates eventually arrived at the residence of the English ambassador – or about-to-be ambassador. This was far superior to Sanderson's leaky dwelling below. Fynes Moryson stayed there in 1597 and described it as being 'upon the top of the hill, in a faire house within a large field and pleasant gardens compassed by a wall'.[108]

Lello was already consumed by impatience when Dallam and his men at last arrived. He had been waiting eighteen months for the organ while his rivals, the Frenchman de Brèves and even the Venetian *bailo*, had outstripped and eclipsed him in influence and prestige. But he was forced to contain himself for two more days. The house, though large, did not have a room high enough to set up the sixteen feet tall organ. A shelter had to be erected in a courtyard. The day after that was a Sunday, and Lello, an intensely religious man, could not allow the crates to be opened. Everyone had to wait.

On Monday 20 August, the entire embassy staff along with a number of 'other gentlemen' invited by Lello to watch, including William Aldridge, the consul on Chios, gathered expectantly in the courtyard.

The result revealed a catastrophe. As Dallam and Harvey levered the top off the first crate with a crowbar there rose a powerful smell of rotting straw. Quite soon, everyone realised that the organ had, to Lello's eyes at least, been irretrievably ruined. The woodwork had fallen apart – 'the glewinge work ... clene Decayed' and Dallam's pipes were 'brused and broken'. It was, he wrote, due to the heat and often violent movement of the sea.

At first appalled, some of the watchers soon became angry. The present was useless, worthless. It wasn't worth twopence. The exchange which followed, Dallam said – as he always did about such exchanges – 'this time I will omitt'. But from what followed one can guess roughly what he said. Lello seems to have been too shattered to speak, but William Aldridge said that if Dallam made it 'perfitt' as he'd said he would, he, Aldridge, would personally give him £15.

'So,' wrote Dallam, 'about my work I wente.'

The Ottomans

Going about their work in Lello's courtyard, Dallam and his three colleagues – Watson the joiner, Buckett the painter, and his engineer John Harvey – could look out over the walls of Galata (still plainly visible in Melchior Lorck's celebrated ink drawing) to the port below and across to the great city of Constantinople opposite. [109]'Perhaps,' wrote William Gelot in 1683, 'altogether the most beautiful prospect in the World.' An Ottoman poet, according to Mansel, described it as a view 'that made heaven gasp with envy.' In fact, it wasn't always – or widely – known as Constantinople. At this time, the Scandinavians called it Micklegarth – City of Great Girth; the Slavs called it Tsarigrad – the Emperor's City; the Arabs called it Dersaâdet – the Abode of Felicity. Istanbul, although not the official name until 1930, was also used, probably from the colloquial Greek *as stin poli,* 'to or in the city'.

[110]Much larger than London in 1600, population estimates vary between 500,000 and 700,000, with variations, too, in the length of the immense and impregnable walls Dallam had seen some of as they sailed in. Built between 412 and 422 AD, the walls embraced and protected the city from the Golden Horn round to the Sea of Marmara – moated, of triple thickness, with 192 towers strategically placed along their winding length, rising and falling, as Mansel says, with the inequalities of the hilly ground. You could still see much of them, crumbling and overgrown, in the nineteenth century. Even now, protected fragments remain. Dallam was to explore the streets inside towards the end of his stay so thoroughly he completely wore through a pair of stout leather shoes. But the power of this empire had begun to grow long before his arrival.

[111]The story is complicated, but put simply can be resolved into a picture of nomadic tribes originally from Mongolia and Central Asia who continually invaded westwards. By 1300, much of Asia Minor was divided into a number of little Turkish principalities, constantly changing, whose chief *raison d'être* was to get loot from raids on the Christian Byzantine lands at their borders and across into the Balkans. This predatory activity was given a sort of dignity and unity by Islam – the aim, that is, to conquer and convert all Christians (whom they would, paradoxically, often call on as temporary allies). Among these little tribes was that of Osman – destined eventually to become a world empire. The Osmans, or Ottomans, saw themselves as unique and far superior to ordinary Turks, indeed not really Turks at all

but a dynasty. 'Turks' was a term they reserved disdainfully for those they saw as Anatolian peasants. This disdain lasted. It was at its strongest in the nineteenth and twentieth centuries leading up to the Republic in 1924.

The Ottomans were indeed unique, and in some interesting ways. Because the main aim of the little tribes, though seemingly spurred by religious idealism, was in fact loot, once they had conquered and looted they had to move on and conquer and loot somewhere else. Conquest, as we are reminded all too clearly today, is not the same as governing. But, alone among the tribes the Ottomans were slowly transformed by the ferocious resistance of the Byzantines – symbolised at the very end of their progress by the defiance of Constantinople behind those tremendous walls. This meant the Ottomans could only advance very slowly. Their conquests lasted because they learnt to govern; they learnt to use the indigenous Christians and Jews to help them do it, and used them to pay taxes and tribute in return for religious toleration.

After that last conquest of the 1,000-year-old Byzantine Empire, Mehmed II, The Conqueror, entered a Constantinople ravaged, burnt and depopulated by looting, plague, slaughter and people fleeing from defeat. To repeople and rebuild prosperity, Mehmed continued the lesson which the Ottomans had already learnt paid off – he encouraged all nationalities to settle and tolerated all religions. And this practice was to spread and continue. It was later calculated that the Ottoman Empire contained seventy-two and a half nationalities (half, because, as Mansel notes, gypsies were allowed half a nationality). [112]But it was after 1453 that Mehmed began to create a multicultural city that was not historically without precedent (in the early Middle Ages, for instance, Khazaria in the Caucasus welcomed all outsiders, not just Jews, but Greek Christians, Muslims, Iranians and pagan Slavs). But Constantinople was still highly unusual. As regards tolerating the various different religions it certainly did not pertain to the views of medieval and post-medieval Europe. Here all sides believed religious uniformity was vital. In the sixteenth century there were virtual bonfires of heretics in

London and Berlin, Slavs massacred them and they were buried alive in the Plaza Major of Madrid. Jews had been expelled from Spain and, in 1290, from England, not allowed back until Cromwell. In Constantinople they were at first forcibly imported, later they came voluntarily in considerable numbers. The same was true of Armenians.

Encouraged by the enlightened *realpolitik* characteristic of the Ottomans for economic reasons, the situation was not without difficulties. They realised that different nations would compete to surpass each other and the state would benefit – but competition led to tensions. These were augmented because each nationality – and in the city ten languages were spoken – tended to congregate in different areas, usually in Galata. There were strict dress regulations lasting until the nineteenth century. Only Muslims, for instance, could wear white or green turbans, compared to Greeks in their blue hats, Armenians in dark blue and Jews in yellow hats (a 'yellow' to find echoes centuries later in Nazi Germany). Orders of this sort were frequently repeated which means they must have been frequently broken. In 1580, for example, Jews and Christians were forbidden to dress like Muslims yet we know for a fact that Burton and later Glover did exactly that – and were esteemed for so doing.

Economic growth resulted, as so often, in extravagant building. After and including Mehmed II, sultan after sultan built ever more beautiful and ambitious mosques which, as Mansel with his usual elegance puts it, 'at once advertised and absolved their wealth.' [113] This wealth followed power, and during the fifteenth and sixteenth centuries Ottoman power became immense. After 1500 they were too strong to need or bother about allies, with the sole exception of naval allies against Spain. Not just Persia and Egypt, but the whole coast from Morocco to Mesopotamia, the lands from Poland to Yemen, owed allegiance to the sultans, and in addition the Ottomans ruled the seas to India. Until the end of the seventeenth century, they were almost continually at war with one European power or another. Under Suleyman the Magnificent (1520–66) their power reached its apogee – in 1526, the Ottomans were within 100 miles of Vienna. The Kings of France begged for the Sultan's help; in 1547, the Hapsburg Holy Roman Empire agreed to pay tribute.

And what is interesting about this development, as with so many Ottoman developments, is that it had its roots in their long history of gradual conquest in Asia Minor and the Balkans. Here, as I said, they had learnt to use the indigenous Christian population both to help govern and to provide taxation, in tandem with both compelling and inviting them into Constantinople (foreign nationals and Jews always paid higher taxes). Having evolved as conquerors, conquering became an aim, a goal – dignified, if that is the word, as before by Islam. A Venetian envoy reported Mehmed II saying 'there must be only one empire, one faith, and one sovereignty in the world. No place is more deserving than Constantinople for the creation of unity in the world.' By the middle of the sixteenth century, Suleyman could say 'I am the Sultan of Sultans, the Sovereign of Sovereigns, the distributor of Crowns to the Monarchs of the globe'. And this assumption, echoing Alexander the Great (and perhaps reviving in some areas of Islam today) that Ottoman Islam should, in fact did, rule the world, clearly made an international, multicultural and multireligious city not only sensible but inevitable. With gold and silver and copper and ivory and slaves, every imaginable form of wealth passing in as booty or tribute from conquests and the threat of conquest, so the instruments of power became powerful, too.

Early in the fourteenth century, the slowly conquering Ottomans took to incorporating new troops from the people they overran into their fighting force. 'New troops' in Turkish is *yeni ceri,* who became the Janissaries' *corbaci.* Renowned for discipline, their ferocity and their courage to the point of disregarding death, by the end of the fifteenth century they numbered 2,000, by the mid-sixteenth century there were 12,000, by 1591 there were 48,088 and they had become the flower of the army, along with the *Spahi* or elite cavalry.[114]

But the Janissaries were not solely soldiers. In a way which to us seems eccentric, the Ottomans often combined domestic with military duties, as we'll see again in a moment with the palace gardeners. Food seems to have been extremely important to the Janissaries. They were divided into ortas of one hundred men each. The commander of every orta had the title of *corbaci* or soup cook and wore a soup ladle at his belt. One or possibly two ortas went further: They did all the cooking for the seraglio, their standard was a cooking pot, their cap badge a rice fork and their ranks named after other kitchen utensils. These crack units were called The Imperial Larder.

The Janissaries were not only renowned for their ferocity and courage but also for the superiority of their weapons. This was true of much earlier Muslim troops, as the Crusaders were well aware. The swords and spears of the Muslims were far sharper and far stronger than anything in the West. [115]The secret of this has recently been discovered. From 900 to 1750, their scimitars and other weapons were forged from an Indian steel called *wootz*. Studied under an electron microscope, *wootz* steel has been found to contain carbon nanotubes and even nanowires. This explains the extraordinary properties of these weapons; far harder to damage, once given an edge weapons of *wootz* steel would retain it in a way no other steel could then do. *Wootz* steel also explains a dramatic passage in one of Walter Scott's novels. Saladin is challenged by Richard the Lionheart to show who has the most powerful sword. The Crusader raises his mighty two-handed sword and cleaves a great block of stone. Smiling, Saladin takes a large satin cushion and calmly slices it in half.[116]

Dallam almost certainly watched contingents of Janissaries when he was on the *Hector* anchored outside Aleppo, as well as witnessing their strength, if only in number, in the weeks he spent in the Topkapi Palace. But what he would have seen directly, since it was right below him along the shores of the Golden Horn, was the Sultan's mighty navy. Despite Lepanto, this was still a fearsome fighting force. As we saw, Elizabeth had several times asked for it to help England against Spain.

[117]The Golden Horn was the only safe port between the Sea of Marmara, notorious for bad weather, and the Black Sea, known as 'the punishing sea'. The Horn was so extensive and so protected that in winter more than 1,000 ships could unload straight to the shore across planks on to the wharves and jetties of both Galata and Eminönü opposite, running below the Topkapi Palace. Fifteen thousand people worked the ports stretching either side and manned the myriad little boats plying between the two cities. They lived in whole villages interspersed with parks and palace gardens, with cemeteries shaded by towering cypresses, dense groves of plane trees and weeping willows and orchards with every kind of fruit – peaches, apricots, quince and pomegranate.

This mini-population served the largest single naval complex in the world at that time, with the imperial arsenal and imperial dockyards. The arsenal sheds could build 200 galleys at a time, with next to them the gunpowder and munition factories. Though not nearly as heavily armed as European ships, galleys still carried formidable weapons at their prow. They were also far faster and far more manoeuvrable than Western ships. They had sails, but their aim was to ram enemy ships and then board them. This was accomplished by their Turkish, Greek and Dalmatian troops, but the galley engines were the slaves captured in war and piracy. Two or three thousand, they lived appalling lives, locked into a huge grey building next to the arsenal, since as well as rowing naked under the lash they also, like prisoners forced to dig their own graves, built the galleys.

[118]Here, too, was the palace of the man who commanded all this – the lord high admiral, the kaptan pasha. Originally Scipio Cicala, he belonged to a noble Genoese family settled in Sicily. Captured with his father by the Turks when young, his father died in prison, but the youth was easily persuaded to embrace Islam and enter the imperial service, and quite quickly rose to become grand admiral. In 1596, he turned an almost inevitable defeat by the Christian army in Hungary by rallying the retreating Turks and leading them to victory beside the Sultan at the battle of Keresztes, not 100 kilometres east

of Budapest. The Grand Signor embraced him and made him grand vizier on the spot, to replace the cowardly vizier who had fled at the beginning of the battle. But he caused anger and resentment by his severe discipline and a month later was reappointed grand admiral, for which he had earlier asked.

So – a hard man. In 1600, he was one of the Sultan's principal officers, and he also had authority over the Aegean Islands and Galata, and was thus doubly important to Lello (who of course, like him, spoke Italian). Cultivated first by Barton before Lello, he was by tradition and the self-interest fuelled by bribes and presents, friendly to England and, in one of the final showdowns with France, was to prove decisive. The point, as I mentioned earlier, was that power lay with those who had the ear of the Sultan (as it does still today with those close to any head of government). Here, it was men like the hoca, the chief eunuch, the head valet and so on. But it was the men who actually governed the empire, the chief justices, the lord treasurer, the viziers – especially, of course, the grand vizier – and the lord high admiral, who had still more substantive power. Another of these was the bostancıbaşı, or head gardener.

It may seem odd that a gardener had great power, but the title is misleading. The bostancıbaşı commanded an elite force, anything between eight and twelve thousand men, separate but equal to the Janissaries, and like them had a combination of military and domestic duties. As well as tending the vast royal gardens, they guarded the city and the seas surrounding it. They rowed the Sultan's kayak, when the leading bostancıbaşı would sit close to the Sultan and converse with him; they controlled the Bosphorus, the Golden Horn and the Sea of Marmara close to the city. At night they patrolled the port in launches and by day, the sea environs, to arrest troublemakers and prevent traders evading customs dues.

A unique force and a unique commander, and the odd thing about all these leading figures is that very few were actually Turkish. This was due to another unique feature of Ottoman governance.

Devshirme – Taking the Young

In fact, the lord high admiral gives us a clue. We have seen how the conquering Osmanis learnt to incorporate some of those they conquered, as they did with Scipio Cicala, into their service. During the fifteenth century this evolved into an institution based, as so often with the Ottomans, on *realpolitik*. Their disdain for 'Turks' extended to actually distrusting them; but in fact they didn't even trust themselves – at least, they were not trusted by their sultans. The solution was to recruit the servants of government from non-Turks. The process was called *devshirme*, or 'gathering'. Boys and youths aged six to sixteen were gathered in large numbers from the rival Christian populations of the Balkans and Anatolia and brought to Constantinople to be slaves (the Koran forbids Muslims to be slaves, though exceptions could be found to this). In Constantinople (and sometimes, later, in outlying farms) they were circumcised, converted to Islam and taught to speak Turkish. They were chosen for their health and good looks. Those so gathered were recruited into the households of the rich and as Bostancis, Janissaries and into the army. In fact, so many Janissaries were Slavs that they spoke Serbo-Croat among themselves, also true of the army. This system was not as cruel as it sounds. The families from whom the youths were taken were, no doubt, often in despair, but not all of them and often not for long. Their sons also entered the civil service and the government and could, and did, rise to the highest positions in the empire – as grand admirals, generals, chief justices and viziers. Of the first forty-eight grand viziers after the conquest in 1453, only fifteen were Turks (one estimate says only twelve). Free to marry, to own property, well-off and sometimes very wealthy, they would look after their families back in their homelands. And in *realpolitik* terms – it worked. The process of *devshirme* removed potential rebels and created loyal Ottomans. Mansel quotes an official in the fifteenth century who noted about the government administration: 'There are few native-speaking Turks in the palace because the Sultan finds himself more faithfully served by Christian converts who have neither hearth nor home nor parents nor friends.' So well could these 'slaves' do, that supposedly bereft families often rejoiced at the good fortune of their kidnapped sons. Many Bosnians, although Muslims (but not native Turks) begged to be made eligible for gathering – and this was allowed. By the end of the sixteenth century this was not all that uncommon. In 1582 Murad III was reported as letting in thousands of acrobats, wrestlers and entertainers from all over the Balkans to reward them for the success of his son's circumcision celebrations.

And the practice of *devshirme*, though not so extensive nor institutionalised in the same way, was not unknown elsewhere. [119]There was a tradition in the Caucasus, for example, of selling their children into slavery. The Tatars of the Crimea regularly invaded Russia, Poland, Hungary and Croatia and brought back thousands of women and children to sell, often in Constantinople. As a result, and as a result of the Ottomans' endless wars, slaves were quite cheap. White slaves, *manluks*, were brought up in families and treated more as adopted children.

There were, however, a very large group of people who were not all that keen on the practice of *devshirme* – and that was the Ottoman Turks of Constantinople themselves. *Devshirme* effectively cut them off from a great many positions of power and wealth in their empire.

[120]The solution – or outlet – was religion. This was an extremely important sphere of society. On the whole, Muslim countries were more openly devout than Western countries. Europeans arriving in Constantinople were astonished at the intense fervour in the mosques compared to their own great churches. [121]Mansel quotes such a visitor, 'No one lounges or walks about in a church, no one chatters with one another and nothing else is heard but fervent prayer.' The same is true today. Where the din of traffic, the rushing and unceasing press of people, the roar of overhead planes dominate our cities, in the towns and cities of Islam, now as then, the call of the *muezzin* echoes across the streets, reminding the people of the God in whom they believe and calling them to worship Him.

The laudable toleration of Christianity might seem more surprising given the intensity of Islamic belief, but in fact the opposite is true. As Mansel perceptively notes, Christians were and are 'people of the book' like Muslims. Their religion might have been overtaken by Islam but it was not alien. Abraham and Mary are revered by Muslims. You will remember that, if it happened, it was to meet 'the prophet Jesus' that Ahmed Çelebi blew himself skywards in 1623. Christians in Constantinople had the station of *zimmi* – protected persons.

A number of things contributed to the importance of their religion among the Ottomans and underpinned it. In Islam, state rule depends on it. Laws are only legitimate if they enforce or agree with the *sheriat,* the holy word of the *Koran*. In Constantinople there was a further element. Other Muslim rulers of the day owed their position to being descended from the Prophet or his tribe, the *Qureish*. The Ottomans owed their position to force. This 'legitimacy deficit', as Mansel calls it, caused a good deal of anxiety. Sultans tried to excel each other in religious fervour (a fact which in the end was to have a bearing on Dallam – or rather the present he had helped make). As soon as they possibly could, in 1459, the Ottomans 'discovered' a significant grave in the city, that of Abu Ayyub, a close companion of the Prophet. In 1517, after Sultan Selim I had added Egypt to the conquest of Syria and the areas in Arabia holding the holy cities of Mecca and Medina, Constantinople became the capital of Islam.

All these factors combined to make the servants of Islam, the learned men, the *ulema,* an extremely significant and powerful element in Constantinople and Ottoman society. The head of the *ulema* was the Mufti. His role was to issue *fatwas* that the Sultan's edicts were in accordance with Muslim law. This was a power totally independent of the Sultan, and this legitimising role was so vital that the Mufti was the third most important person in the empire after the grand vizier and the Sultan himself. The embarrassment of Lello about Barton's very large debt to this important figure, still unpaid long after Barton's death, was understandably very considerable.

A final level of economic and social organisation cemented the role of the *ulema* and made their position even more desirable to the Turkish citizens of Constantinople. Not only were the Ottomans far more tolerant of other races and other religions than Westerners, their charity was far more effective. Mosques were central here, too. Round the Fatih Mosque, for instance, an entire complex grew up; a hospice for dervishes, an inn for travellers, a hospital that provided patients with two meals a day – often delicious, of pheasant and partridge – and a soup kitchen distributing food to the poor. Over 1,000 people a day were fed at Fatih, and this pattern was echoed all over Constantinople and across the dominions. This was a people who, as Mansel notes, not only created a dynastic empire but a system of social welfare. And what is extraordinary is how long it lasted. Two hundred years later, in the eighteenth century, it was estimated that Constantinople was feeding 30,000 a day. Apart from kindness, it was another essay in *realpolitik* – a hungry population, as France showed in 1789, is a dangerous population.

The mosques and their attendant welfare complexes were very well endowed, as universities and their colleges used to be and sometimes still are in Britain. The Fatih for instance, described above, was endowed with property, like the nearby leather and saddle market with 110 shops. Staffed by considerable numbers of *ulema*, here were the careers sought after by the Muslims of Constantinople; to become *imams,* and lead prayers; *sheikhs* and deliver sermons; *muezzins* and call the faithful to prayer and scholars. Below these elevated callings of *sheikhs* and scholars *ulema* were more humble roles – doormen, lesson readers, supervisors of ablutions and baths and other charitable dogsbodies like cooks and cleaners. But for the population at large, the appeal of the jobs surrounding the *ulema*, apart from the prestige, were the salaries. Their descendants could inherit the right to administer and receive these salaries, and this continued into the twentieth century.

This very brief historical survey of that fascinating civilisation, especially as it was manifested in Constantinople in 1600, while essential to understand

and imagine what Dallam had found himself in, was only in a vague and general way appreciated by the young craftsman himself. Dallam knew, of course – it was common and frightened knowledge across the West – that he had come to a very powerful empire to which his queen felt she had to send lavish gifts. He was surrounded by visible signs of its wealth and might. His companions and his superiors talked about it. Nevertheless, judging from his diary, his awareness was just that – vague and general. Something which touched him much more sharply and which he frequently mentions and to which he sometimes reacted dramatically, was the final expression of all the elements I have outlined, and this was the sudden, arbitrary, often terrifyingly cruel demonstration of the Sultan's absolute and despotic power.

Power, Death and Cruelty

[122]When Gentile Bellini was sent to the palace of Mehmed II in 1479 by Venice, at the Sultan's request, he painted the now famous portrait a few months before Mehmed died. He also showed him a painting of John the Baptist's severed head. Mehmed, who had no doubt seen a good number of severed heads, was scornful. The picture was completely inaccurate. To prove it, he had a servant brought in and, to the painter's horror, had him decapitated on the spot.

It might be thought this was an example, common throughout history, of how often in slave societies, which Constantinople was, slaves are treated as less than human. But in fact, as we've seen, all the Sultan's most important servants were, in origin, technically slaves, yet they could reach the most powerful and wealthy positions in the empire. [123]One such, Grand Vizier Sokollu Mehmed Pasha (1565–79), paid for the construction of 300 mosques, had four palaces in Constantinople, a 360-room palace in Edirne and, when he died, 18 million gold *piastres*. He passed all this on to his son and founded a dynasty. He had served and survived three sultans.

Perhaps he was lucky to die in his bed, because he and all the immensely rich and immensely powerful ministers and servants like him could be destroyed at the stamp of a petulant slipper. The Sultan's God-given power of life and death over all his servants, over his slaves and over his family, was absolute. The signal and the result were swift. If he opened a window in the Tower of Justice just above the divan chamber or stamped his foot when talking with someone, mutes (usually) would spring forth and strangle, decapitate or stab whoever it was to death. Grand viziers were sometimes dispatched by the Sultan himself. Suddenly, a foot moved. At once, wrote Naima, in a passage quoted by Mansel, 'the emperor drew his sword and cut his throat'. [124]In 1606, Grand Vizier Dervish Pasha was strangled by imperial gardeners. So absolute was this power and so long had it existed, that very few objected to their deaths. The victims would sometimes sign the writs of accusations which would later be attached to their remains.

[125]Nor were these arbitrary executions rare. Philippe du Fresne-Canaya noted, in the 1550s, that in the Chamber of Petitions, lurking behind the walls, 'were hidden I don't know how many mutes, who are the most loyal and the most experienced executioners of the atrocious commandments of their tyrant'. He stamped his foot if anything displeased him – and he did this frequently.

[126]There were a good many contemporary Turkish proverbs pertaining to this state of affairs, none condemning. In fact, they have an air of secret satisfaction. 'The neck of a servant of the Sultan is thinner than a hair's breadth.' 'He that is even the greatest in office is but a statue of glass.' Yet these in some ways precarious figures had the same arbitrary power as their Sultan. [127]A Turk found drunk in the streets during Ramadan was at once hauled before the grand vizier who, 'without giving him any respite for the recovery of his wits, caused a ladleful of boiling lead to be poured down his throat, wherewith the wretch perished immediately'.

One might wonder, incidentally, at that lack of condemnation in the proverbs and indeed in the populace generally. As far as the people of Constantinople went, there were two considerable motives for acquiescence. The vast majority of the victims were not close to them, not Turks. They were the products of *devshirme*. And second, the people, like those governed everywhere, often felt that those governing them were corrupt vultures, intent on cheating them and stealing from them. They were pleased to see their Sultan standing up for them and eliminating such rogues.

The Ottomans used appalling tortures to punish and in pursuit of justice. Orhan Pamuk, whose wonderful novel, *My Name is Red*, set in Constantinople more or less exactly in Dallam's time there, is precise about Ottoman torture. But we should see all this in the context of those savage centuries. [128]Apart from the arbitrary nature and the frequency of their exercise of despotic power, which did shock contemporaries, the Ottomans were not really all that much worse than other nations at that time – who were sometimes not different in those aspects either.

An anonymous author, quoted by Sarah Bradford in her admirable book on Lucrezia Borgia, wrote of Cesare Borgia, 'Who from being a Cardinal has made himself into an assassin. He lives like the Turks, surrounded by a flock of prostitutes, guarded by armed soldiers. At his order or decree men are killed, wounded, thrown into the Tiber, poisoned, despoiled of all their possessions.' But other princes of the time, and not just in Italy, behaved nearly as ruthlessly.

Torture was universal all over Europe. In England it was not permitted by common law, though in Elizabeth's reign special powers were invoked to justify its use for exhorting information from Catholics suspected of treason. But even the routine execution of criminals – not to mention the burning alive of hundreds of heretics – could be terrible. Hanging was not hanging as practised here until the mid-twentieth century, which resulted in instantaneous death as the neck was broken, but was in effect throttling. The friends of someone hanged would often pull on the victim's feet to try and speed up the process.

Hanged, drawn and quartered was not just a phrase; it described an appalling torture, usually, but not always, reserved for heretics. For example, in 1586 those implicated in the Babington Plot to assassinate the queen were executed in this way, with the addition of their genitals being hacked off before their eyes. The victims were cut down before they were dead and, even if unconscious, could go on to suffer atrocious agonies. [129]There is an account of the death of a Catholic priest, Hugh Green, in August 1642. He was cut down unconscious but 'the man who was to quarter him,' wrote Elizabeth Willoughby, who attended him, 'was so long dismembering him that he came to his perfect senses.' She goes on, 'Then did this butcher cut his belly on both sides, and turn the flap upon his breast, which the holy man feeling put his left hand upon his bowels, and looking on his bloody hand laid it down by his side, and lifting up his right hand he crossed himself, saying three times, Jesu, Jesu, Jesu Mercy. The which, although unworthy, I am a witness of, for my hand was on his forehead ... all the Catholics were pressed away from him by the unruly multitude except myself ... Whilst he was thus calling upon Jesus, the butcher did pull a piece of his liver out instead of his heart, and tumbling his guts out every way to see if his heart was not among them, then with his knife he raked in the body ... Methought my heart was pulled out of my body to see him in such cruel pains, lifting up his eyes to heaven, and not yet dead. Then I could not longer hold, but cried out upon them that did so torment him. His forehead was bathed in sweat, and blood and water flowed from his eyes and nose. And when on account of the gushing streams of blood his tongue could no longer pronounce the saving name of Jesus, his lips moved, and the frequent groans which he uttered from his inmost heart were proof of the most bitter pain and torture which he suffered.'

Such examples of Western brutality could be matched in all countries before and after 1600 – and then continued for hundreds of years. It is not easy to say the Ottomans were much worse. [130]Casanova has a vivid description of the terrible death of Damiens in 1757 for attempting to assassinate Louis XV. Damiens was skinned alive on scaffolding in front of an enormous baying crowd. Casanova's description of the actual flaying is brief. What really interested him far more, and which he describes in detail, is that in the press of people he'd invited to watch the grisly show from a hired room, his young and clearly very virile friend Count Tiretta stood very close behind a middle-aged woman who Casanova tactfully calls Madame XXX (this was because she was the aunt of his current love, whom he tactfully refers to as Mademoiselle de la M.... Re). The niece describes her aunt, irritatingly and ostentatiously devout, with rheumy eyes and bad breath, as 'hideous'. Anxious not to tread on Madame XXX's long dress, Tiretta raised it up, raised it up so high that he could, and then did, make love to her from behind. Partly concealed by her voluminous skirts and under cover of Damiens' shrieks, he continued to do this for the two hours it took Damiens to die. The niece supposed that her aunt would have been appalled and disgusted by what was happening and only didn't cry out for fear of exposure to those crowded round her. In fact, she enjoyed it so much that, at some cost, she hired Count Tiretta to come and live with her for a year.

But from our point of view, how much of specifically Ottoman behaviour and practice was Dallam aware of? The answer must be a good deal.

The Ottomans were notorious in England for their cruelty and the arbitrary nature of its expression. In Elizabeth's court, and from there soon out into London itself, news of the frequent executions in Constantinople were reported with thrilling horror. It was often not the execution which shocked the Elizabethans so much as their manner. [131]On 28 May 1595, for instance, news came that a baker had been cooked in his own oven for using false weights.

The point is that there was widespread popular prejudice against Islam/ Turks/Ottomans (interchangeable in this context), which derived ultimately from the Crusades and the centuries of opprobrium heaped on Saracens. The Turk was the enemy, the evil. [132]At the Siege of Malta by Suleyman the Magnificent, prayers were said all over England. There were little 'bokes of prayer against the Turke bought everywhere ... 2d. Cantery [Canterbury] bought 3 such bokes'. The evil Turk appeared in plays by Marlowe and Shakespeare, as I mentioned earlier. The cruel Turk was the mainstay of religious tracts and sermons, which were, as James Mather writes in his *Pashas: Traders and Travellers in the Islamic World*, a crude 'recycling of a bigoted medieval inheritance'.[133]

Dallam would have known a good deal of all this and it is important to emphasise it since it explains several of his diary entries. And it would have been much reinforced by his companions on the *Hector* as they got nearer and nearer to the dreaded empire, probably, as I mentioned earlier, from Humphrey Conisby, a fellow traveller, who had made his own translation of Soranzo's frightening portrait of Mehmed III.[134]

It was the believed licentiousness that added the final tone to the popular condemnation – the *harem*, the seraglio, the single function in the palace by which, as we saw, the entire city, almost the entire people, were known. The pleasure of moral disapproval contained, as often, a strong element of envy.

In a few days, Dallam was to penetrate deeper into the actual seraglio than any Christian before him or any Christian for hundreds of years after him. But first came the dramatic start in Lello's campaign to win back influence with the Sultan and his government.

Lello's Campaign

On 28 August, the *Hector* sailed forth on to the Sea of Marmara and, sounding her trumpets, passed serenely before the Pearl Kiosk. The kiosks were a number of miniature palaces in the Topkapi grounds where the sultans liked to pass time with their courts and concubines. [135]This one was sited on the old Byzantine sea wall facing the Marmara and the Bosphorus. Here the *Hector* anchored, watched with considerable curiosity by Mehmed III and some of his courtiers.

The ship looked splendid in the bright summer sun. Dallam, showing off his new expert knowledge, describes how every mast was new painted and from every mast pennants streamed in the breeze – from 'mayne top, foretop, myssen top, sprid saile top … '. Her 'fights' were out, canvas screens hung amid ships to hide the men from the enemy, but now brightly coloured.

Lello claimed in a letter to Cecil that he had ordered this transformation, but it is clear from Dallam that Parsons, who knew exactly what was wanted, had begun on this, as we noted, as soon as the *Hector* arrived. The trouble was, Lello had lost all faith in the organ – though its repair was nearing completion. He reported how 'evill handed' it had been on the voyage, a failure made worse because the whole of Constantinople was talking about it. 'Except the plate and the coatche, the rest of the presente is of small esteeme.' [136]Indeed, according to the Venetian *bailo*, still more of the present, suits and cloth 'are all mouldy and ruined'. And, in any case, the coach was already promised to the old Sultana, the valide, who was so excited she had sent two horses to Galata at *once* to collect it, irritating Lello since he had to feed and stable them while the coach, too, was repaired and repainted. Lello felt he was relying almost entirely on the impression made by the *Hector*.

And, at last, he was not disappointed. The bombardment, for such it seemed, began with the discharge of all twenty-seven cannon, followed by the firing in unison of muskets from the men packing the top decks, each pause followed again and then again, and then again by the massive explosion of the great cast-iron, 7,000 lb culverins, the demi-culverins, the sakers and minions, and between each colossal discharge, echoing across Constantinople, sending smoke billowing out over the Bosphorus and the Sea of Marmara, came again 'a vallie of smale shott'. And it was done, said Dallam, with perfect timing.

It is difficult from Dallam to tell how long the show went on. He says they discharged 'eighte score great shotte', which is 120 times. He doesn't say if they fired a rolling relay, each gun following another, or in unison. It was almost certainly the second. There were twenty-seven 'great shotte', and each time it took about ten minutes for the bigger guns to cool down (they were cooled with vinegar, whose rapid evaporation made it highly effective for this task,[137] vinegar which, incidentally, Dallam used to clean his organ pipes) and they had then to be recharged. A rolling relay would have gone on far too long. With the big guns firing in unison, it would have meant six separate salvoes, taking something over half an hour, which is about what one would expect.

Whichever it was, the whole show was a huge success. A success which continued to reverberate for days afterwards. So intrigued was the Sultan that he sent two men on to the *Hector* to see how many guns she had. He had, it seemed, thought eighty. He was amazed to learn that such power was generated by only twenty-seven cannon. A few days later, on 2 September, he slipped secretly out of the Kiosk and rowed round and round the ship so that he could look at her himself. An hour later, the queen mother, the valide, did the same.

In fact, everything pleased the Sultan. 'The sounds of our Inglishe trumpettes,' Lello wrote to Cecil, 'gave him so great contente, as those aboute him saye they have not seen him so delight in any Christian princes strength and defense.' And that was the whole point of the exercise. As the *bailo*, Girolamo Cappello, grudgingly admitted in his dispatch to the Doge and Senate, the Turks greatly valued an alliance with England 'which they think is highly important for holding the King of Spain in check'.

[138]Cappello's memoranda to the Doge are often amusing but – irritated by Lello's success, the first in months – adds in his dispatch of 15 September 1599, 'English vanity in showing off this ship and its armament, which they allow anyone who goes on board to see, will do harm to Christendom and open the eyes of the Turks to things they do not know.' The Turks, of course, knew all about what they saw perfectly well already, but the more it was reenforced the better.

But the bombardment did cause one, possibly even two, tragedies. [139]The gunpowder for the culverins was packed into cartridges, each holding the correct amount of powder for each type of gun. Unwrapped gunpowder was not allowed to be handled on deck. There was one danger, apart from the barrel bursting. The guns could get extremely hot with repeated firing, when they were cooled with vinegar, but very occasionally fire would remain at the bottom of the barrel and this could ignite a cartridge prematurely. This happened at the very end of the salute to the Sultan. 'One of the stouteste sailors in the ship,' wrote Dallam, rammed home his cartridge into one of the big culverins – and it instantly exploded, blowing 'that man quite awaye in the smoke'. His legs and waist were later found two miles away, 'his heade in another place'.

A second man, the ship's carpenter, was sick in bed and 'wyth the reporte of the first greate peece that was discharged he died'.

These deaths convinced Dallam, showing how he shared the common European prejudice against the Turks, that they were a punishment for the evil of bestowing 'this great trumpte and charge on an infidel'. But it was to work at wooing that infidel, as soon as his organ was ready, that he was to spend much of the rest of his time in Constantinople.

The Gifts

It took Dallam and his team a further three days after the *Hector*'s salute to the Sultan to finally finish repairing the organ. He gives no details of this and the only problem might have been glue. [140]Fish glue, which he would have preferred, since, in contrast to animal glue from hooves or hide, it could be applied on top of old glue, only came to England in the mid-sixteenth century. Oddly enough it seems not yet to have been discovered in Constantinople, even though it was used in Egypt 3,500 years ago. But fish were plentiful and the glue was easily made from them by boiling down the flesh, offal and bones.

Lello had told Cecil that the whole of Constantinople was talking about the organ, and it was clearly true. As Dallam relates, a stream of distinguished visitors poured in to look at it. The King of Fez, with one of whose wives, as we saw, Barton may have had an affair, had already been to see it on 23 August and had sat watching Dallam working on it for half a day. He came again on 27 August (the Fez royal family had been driven into exile by the Emperor of Morocco fifty years before). On Tuesday 4 September, a figure Mayes calls the qapu asha (and Dallam the cappagaw) came to see the organ.

Mayes says this was the chief white eunuch and makes him lord chamberlain and the Sultan's private secretary (in fact the chief black eunuch, the kizlar aga, was a more powerful figure). On Friday 7 September, the bostancibasi, chief gardener and chief of much else, already a Lello supporter, came. That same evening, all these figures, now including the grand vizier (who was also, it happened, the Sultan's brother-in-law) were entertained together in the embassy – and no doubt once again saw the organ. Dallam does not say he activated it, so they could only report back to the Sultan, which they certainly did, its impressive appearance and not describe its alleged wonders.

And none of them, then or thereafter, called it an organ. Various historians have said this was because the Ottamans didn't have a word for organ (or not until the 1630s). [141]This is true, as far as it goes; but they did have words designating 'musical instrument' – for instance *sâz* and *arganûn* (found in a text c.1500). One would expect they would use 'musical instrument' to describe what was exactly that. But in fact they called it a clock. The reason was that, just as the Levant merchants had expected, it was the various clockwork marvels (if they *were* clockwork – we'll come to this) which fascinated and impressed them – something, as regards the clock, no doubt augmented because it also incorporated the movements of the planets. Astrology was as important to the Ottomans as it was everywhere then. But *everyone,* apart from the English, referred to the organ as a clock. [142]On 15 September 1599, the *bailo* describes it as 'an organ very cunningly designed, which serves as a clock'. By October and thereafter he simply calls it a clock. And a clock it remained. [143]Mustapha bin Ibrahim Safi, for example, Ahmed I's imam, an Ottoman historian working later but not all that much later, wrote, '... a woman, Queen of a sizeable kingdom – sent as a gift a masterpiece of craftsmanship, a clock.'

[144]All the distinguished visitors to see the organ had praised it and said they were sure the Sultan would be delighted. Lello's confidence was boosted – but not much. As a character, he was clearly highly nervous. His unnecessary dispatch of a boat down the Dardanelles to collect Dallam,

Glover and the rest because the *Hector* was delayed alone shows that. What else do we know of him? Mayes describes him as 'tall and thin, awkward in his bearing, nervous ... he spoke in a high-pitched voice and was given to blushing'. His nickname was 'fogge'. This, including the nickname fog, is (roughly) derived from a letter written by John Kitely, the embassy doctor. But the letter was to Sanderson, who quotes it. In fact every single critical comment about Lello comes from Sanderson, and has been accepted and passed on by historians ever since. Later, he quotes a letter from John Ker to him, which says the 'wante of spirite and corage [in Lello] both made the creditie of th'English nation to hange the heade and blushe at the open reproaches and scornes of th'other nations'. But you have to watch it with Sanderson. He criticises everyone, usually viciously. He disliked Lello intensely, describing him as 'faulse' and insincere. By the end of Lello's tenure in 1608, they weren't speaking to each other. Sanderson was also jealous of the amount of money Lello made in private trading (which they all did, including Sanderson himself).

But there are other views. Paul Pindar, for example, praised Lello's behaviour with the Sultan. The clergyman William Biddulph, the subject of Gerald MacLean's second penetrating and lively study, was Lello's chaplain for a while. He praises his courage and his 'religious carriage and unspotted life' (something which couldn't be applied to Biddulph's own life). He also said that had Lello not been ambassador at a particularly difficult time, he would have done better than Barton.

And some of Sanderson's own diatribes can also be differently interpreted. In December 1600, for instance, he reports that Grand Vizier Hafiz Ahmed Pasha said that Lello was an infidel 'wourse than a knave', a madman, a 'fantastical foole ... a hogge not capable of any reason'. The reason for this outburst was that Lello was obstinately demanding concessions for the English which clearly infuriated him but which, when Hafiz fell, he obtained. And, though it is true Lello was, no doubt, greatly helped by his very able assistants, Paul Pindar and Thomas Glover, both of whom later became ambassadors to

Constantinople, in the end his tenure of nearly ten years was a resounding success, for which, as Biddulph noted, he was justly knighted.

But any success seemed to Lello and others quite impossible in September 1599. He thought the praise his visitors lavished on the 'clock' was mostly oriental politeness. He still wished he could give the coach to the Sultan and not the valide (it had cost £600, even more than the organ). His anxieties mounted to a crescendo as the dreaded day, when the Sultan would see the organ, actually approached.

However, he tried to do something to calm himself now by distributing presents to all the chief figures of influence – some, like the Sultan's old tutor, not obviously powerful. These consisted of rolls of valuable cloth and silver or, in special cases like the grand vizier, silver-gilt plate; the mufti, of course, was also specially favoured, which, Lello said to Cecil, he hoped would stop 'the mouthe of the Mufti att the present from further demanding of the money owinge by Mr Barton'.

As we saw much earlier in a brief foray into diplomatic gifts, these had been common for millennia and still are today. What was unusual, and what made dealing with the Ottomans was the necessity to give presents to so many at court.

The mufti's gift may have temporarily stopped his mouth. It didn't stop his resentment. One of the things that was irritating the (Catholic) French and Venetians was the intensely religious Lello's determination to set up a Protestant (which they called Lutheran) church in Galata 'for the use,' the *bailo* wrote, 'of a preaching minister he has brought with him.'[145] The *bailo* planned to ask the Grand Signor (the Sultan) if he could thwart this plan and, together with the French ambassador, went to the mufti, who 'promised us every support'.

Lello, at the urging of the *bailo*, was eventually to abandon his plan in order to pacify his two rivals, but at the time it was rumoured that the queen mother, the valide, had saved him.

Safiye, Mehmed III's mother (and so the valide), received her coach, accompanied (temporarily) by Ned Hall on 11 September. Lello sent one of his two gifted assistants, Paul Pindar, to present it to her. The valide loved the coach. She was so pleased with it that she gave Ned Hall forty gold zecchini (if you follow Mayes – fifty if you follow Sanderson). She also, Lello told Cecil, took the Sultan out in it 'often tymes ... abroade'. She asked Lello for a portrait of Queen Elizabeth and he got Rowland Buckett to paint one from the template sent out with the *Hector* (a suitably flattering template was sent out with all expeditions of this sort).

But the valide not only fell in love with her coach, she also seems to have fallen in love with Paul Pindar. This rumour was so strong that Dallam picked it up: 'The Sultana,' he wrote, 'did take a greate lykinge to Mr Pindar and after wardes she sent for him to have his private companye ...' It is certainly possible, given the very free and indulgent atmosphere prevailing. [146]She was in her late forties, and Pindar was thirty-three or thirty-four. He was clever, shrewd and good looking. His father had wanted him to go to university, but Pindar had decided quite young that he wanted to be rich. It was soon clear that he had a gift for business, and when he was eighteen he went to Venice as his father's factor. For fifteen years he learnt the graces and skills of a sophisticated Italian city. He spoke Italian – and did indeed become very rich. The Sultana Safiye sent him three suits of cloth and 300 gold zecchini after delivering the coach. But we hear no more about her love. Dallam says their attempted meetings were 'croste'. He doesn't say why. Either side could have thought such a liaison might be tricky. Or perhaps her love was just a rumour engendered by the unusual munificence of her gifts (her munificence to Pindar perhaps not all that unusual, but to coachman Ned Hall highly unusual).

But there was no doubt about her power and influence. [147]Nurbanu, the mother of Murad III, was the first of the powerful valides and set the tone for those who came after. Tall, dark-eyed and beautiful, she was enormously wealthy, her stipend from the State Treasury was three times that of the Sultan himself, not to speak of the presents and bribes she got from her position of power. Even though she lived in a palace outside the city walls, she controlled the harem from her lavish apartments inside it. Control of the harem meant even more immediate access to the Sultan than she had anyway and was the secret of real influence. 'All good and evil,' ran a proverb 'comes from the Queen Mother.' Nurbanu negotiated important aspects of foreign policy, and she even commissioned the imperial architect Sinan to build a mosque. The Atik Valide Cami above Üsküdar also comprised the usual complex of baths, hospital and soup kitchen for the poor.

Safiye's power did not equal Nurbanu's – but it was very considerable. She too built, or rather started to build, a mosque, and this, exceptionally, was inside the city walls. She died in 1605 before it was completed, which it finally was in 1665, and the Valide Mosque still dominates the square at Eminönü.

Whether or not her affair with Pindar ended satisfactorily (or even existed), Safiye's support for England did not waver. She told Lello, who told Cecil, she was 'ready to doe all the service she could for [the queen] and our naton'. This may have extended to murder. A few days after the arrival of the coach, the mufti suddenly dropped dead. Everyone thought he had been poisoned on the orders of Safiye to help the English – which it certainly did. Barton's huge debt at last became irrelevant. It meant, in effect, the end of the affair mufti. [148]Sanderson wrote, 'Now I know their wilbe no more words of the seven load of mony he demanded.'

The mothers of the sultans, the valides, were technically concubines. The affection and respect for them, certainly in the cases of Murad III and Mehmed III, were evident – and it was from this their position and power ultimately derived. This fact, and the whole institution of the Constantinople harem, is interesting. It was, along with *deshirme,* in several ways unique to Ottoman civilisation.

It was deep into the harem – deeper, as I've said, than any Christian or Westerner had been before and would be for 200 years after – that Dallam was now about to be immersed.

CHAPTER 5

Climax

In the Topkapi and Assembling the Organ

[149]On Saturday 5th September 1599 Dallam and his team began to dismantle the organ and once again pack it into crates. It took three days, and on Tuesday the 11th, the crates were carried down from the embassy, loaded onto lighters and ferried across the Golden Horn. Dallam was about to see inside the palace whose outline he had looked out on for over three weeks from the vines of Pera. It is clear from his fairly detailed account that this first entry with the crates was through the main gate, the Imperial Gate, a lofty edifice of grey marble.

Just through this, though Dallam doesn't comment on it, he would have seen the heads of those viziers and pashas executed as enemies of the state or for various crimes and misdemeanours (or just at the whim of the Sultan) displayed on marble pillars. Outside the gate, in niches, were the heads of lower figures and often, since so many had been executed, just piles of noses, ears and tongues. He didn't comment on this grisly sight, no doubt because this practice was not unusual all over Europe – if not in such large numbers. In London, for example, as noted earlier, the heads of those hanged or beheaded were boiled and stuck on pikes along London Bridge.

[150]Above the Imperial Gate was an inscription from the Koran which compared it to the gates leading into paradise and, once through, it did seem

to Dallam almost paradisal. The Topkapi Palace, as it became known (one of its sixteen gates was the Topkapi or 'cannon gate'), is set on the extensive raised ground at the eastern end of the Constantinople peninsula, looking out over the Sea of Marmara, the Bosphorus and the Golden Horn. It didn't, and doesn't, remotely resemble Western palaces.

It is arranged as a series of vast courtyards or open spaces, edged by not particularly distinguished and mostly quite low administrative and other buildings. And aspects of this paradise struck Dallam immediately – the beauty of the gardens and the profusion of trees; cypresses (20,000 throughout the palace according to Evliya Çelebi writing in the early seventeenth century), plane trees, weeping willows, pines ... and water. Mohamed's religion rose and spread through the Middle-Eastern countries where the high temperatures can be terrible. Hours in the searing heat, 'the emptiness, the ascetic rigour, the inherent mysticism,' wrote Fernand Braudel, 'the devotion to the implacable sun ... led all over Islam to a longing for the music, the coolness, of running water.' The vast spaces of the Topkapi, as with the confined ones of the Alhambra in Granada, resounded to gushing fountains, the splash of pools, the rippling rills of artificial little streams.

The administrative buildings, round the edge of this first tree-filled space, where anyone could go, included the outer offices of the household, stabling for 4,000 horses, the mint, a hospital and a weapon store 'housed', as Philip Mansel puts it with his usual graceful irony, 'in the ancient Byzantine church of St Irene, dedicated to peace'. As well as numerous gardeners, the Bostancis, working on the flower beds and the lawns, and richly clad soldiers and courtiers strolling about, there might be a few exotic animals – a leopard, an elephant – exercising on leashes. The Sultan was known to go hunting in these great spaces. Occasionally he would watch staged fights between, say, a lion and a buffalo.

As they reached the second gate, although their business was perfectly well known, Dallam's interpreter had to call out what it was before they could pass. (Interpreters were generally Armenians, Italians or Jews. [151]Dallam's, somewhat unusually, was a Cornishman. He called him his 'drugamen'.)

This second gate was the Gate of Salutation and only the Sultan was permitted to ride through it. The second courtyard was even larger than the first and, like it, filled with trees, flowers and the sound of running water. Dallam noticed in particular the grapes, for which he had an almost inordinate appetite. To the left was the Imperial Divan, one of the most powerful buildings in Europe. Here the grand vizier and other viziers and pashas debated policy and decided lawsuits. Ottoman justice was descended from the Byzantine. It was not, as one might expect, complicated and slow, but extremely rapid. Anyone could present a case, and it would be decided immediately, on the spot.

Opposite the Imperial Divan, was a further range of low, undistinguished-looking buildings: accommodation for some of the court and the immense kitchens to feed them (from where Dallam's meals would soon come). These kitchens were able to serve 12,000 people at a time. Simple meals, no doubt, and a feat that can actually be surpassed today (the Golden Temple of Amritsar in India, for instance, feeds 30,000 free every day),[152] but it gives some idea of the size of the Sultan's court. Three thousand pages served the Sultan, his high officials and the harem, according to Evliya Çelebi, and 1,200 bostanicis guarded the palace and tended the gardens. In all, 40,000 people were inside the walls. It was not so much a palace as a small city.

And now Dallam, his crates and his interpreter approached the gate at the end of the second courtyard – the Bab-i Ali or High Gate. It was this gate that foreigners called the Sublime Porte and used as a synonym for the whole Ottoman government. It was later called Bab-i Saadet which is, precisely, Sublime Porte. It was (and still is) colonnaded, with the wide projecting roof often found in Turkish architecture. It was here that the Sultan's throne was placed to mark great Muslim religious festivals.

And passing through this, Dallam was approaching what can be seen as the whole point and aim of the palace – the royal residence. One way of looking at the Topkapi layout is to see it as an enormous military encampment arranged, as it was on campaigns, to increasingly protect and hide the figure at its apex and centre – the Sultan.

Tudor and Valois courts at this time were, compared to that of the Topkapi, relatively informal. Courtiers bowed and kissed the monarch's hand, and procedures were observed, as were hierarchies and politenesses. In Constantinople, deference to the Sultan was total. Courtiers, and even ambassadors, prostrated themselves flat on their faces before him. Then, depending on rank, they were permitted to kiss his hand, lying motionless on a knee, the hem of his kaftan or even just the tip of a hanging sleeve. They departed walking backwards. It was forbidden to sit on a similar seat to the Sultan's, and obviously not on the same seat, however spacious.

And, as you approached the Sultan, there was a deepening silence. Silence reigned in both the second and the third courtyards. Attendants walked on tiptoe and either whispered or conversed in sign language. The silence was so deep, says Mansel, that it created a sense of 'imminent drama'. Even the Janissaries, often drawn up 6,000 strong and, wrote Baron Wratislav in 1591, 'furious and licentious people in war, stood silent and motionless as if they had been hewn out of marble'.

Dallam was well aware of the overwhelming presence of Janissary armed might, and would certainly have noticed the ominous and all-pervading silence, both augmenting his fear of the Sultan. What he probably didn't notice was something far more trivial but which is in fact very germane, even central, to our story – and that was the absence of clocks in the Topkapi.

[153]Time is of enormous importance in the Islamic faith. This is because worshippers are enjoined to say their prayers five times a day, kneeling to face Mecca. The Koran says, 'Do not delay in performing your prayers'. This might well have originally been a simple injunction against slackness, but it is taken it to mean that the *times* of praying must be absolutely correct. Prayers have to be at exact intervals from sunrise to sunset. The Islamic new day begins at sunset, when the old day dies. And, of course, since the sun

rises and sets at different times each day and each season and differently depending on where you are, the times of prayer change continually within all these parameters. And not just the times of prayer, but the times of religious holidays and times and days of fasting. All this is controlled by the position of the sun and the moon.

Turkish time was flexible – or at least it was in the sixteenth century and for long afterwards. Sule Gürbüz, a scholar of timepieces, sees a mystical quality here:

[154]'Actually, this is a more subtle measurement, quite at odds with the strict, unforgiving European time, which cannot endure change in anything. The adolescent stubbornness of European time contrasts with the wise, forbearing Turkish time, which could tolerate each day differently and accept what each day brought. Turkish time was also far more delicate and fragile. European time takes no account of earth or sky, when sternly declaring the hour; with its fixed turning points and constant focus on the unchanging nature of life. Since the human spirit is not fixed, there is a hurtful quality in this view of time.'

Now, to the considerable relief of travellers, Turkish time has been dragooned into European time.

When Dallam was in Constantinople, days were divided according to the time of worship set by the muezzin's call to prayer. Everyone was supposed to be awake at the time of morning prayer, calculated to be when the sun was five degrees above the horizon. Sleeping late was not acceptable. (In books of this time people who slept late were described disapprovingly as 'fermenting'.)

Three instruments were used to calculate the time. The first was the quadrant, a quarter circle of wood divided into lines every five degrees from 0–90°. With this it was possible to measure the angular elevation of the sun and moon above the horizon. Sundials were the second instrument, often set vertically in a wall orientated by compass to face Mecca. And thirdly, since the sun isn't always visible, these two were augmented by sand and water devices, where fixed quantities of either drain away (with water, it was a 'clepsydra' – a stealer of water).

[155]So in the Topkapi in 1600 there were virtually no clocks at all, certainly none in use. And this was true throughout Constantinople. Not that clocks were unknown. The great Turkish astronomer, mathematician and astrologer Takiyüddin bin Maruf el Rásid does seem to have built a clock (which indicated the times of prayer) and certainly wrote the only Ottoman book on clockmaking in 1556, but he had to use the collection of European clocks built up by Grand Vizier Semiz Ali Pasha (nicknamed 'Fleshy')[156] in 1578. Certainly, during the seventeenth century clocks began to appear, though still nearly all European.

But the fact that clocks were known about and could have fairly easily been obtained, at least by the Topkapi, the rich, the mosques, and for public places, shows that their suppression, which is what it amounted to, was deliberate. The moderate expertise required to operate a quadrant and the various sand and water devices kept the power over time in the hands of the ulema. In just the same way, Catholic priests had opposed the translation of the bible so that only those who could read Latin could understand it. As a result, even though it was possible with an almanac to see with clocks when prayer times were throughout the year, quadrants and sundials went on being used and installed throughout the seventeenth century and into the eighteenth century. A new vertical sundial was built into the wall of the Mihrimah Sultan Mosque in Üsküdar in 1769.

All this partly explains the fascination already aroused by Dallam's clock-organ in 1599 and why it was called a clock. It was not just the clock function, of course, but the whole ingenious mechanical array which impressed and delighted them – but the clock, with its attendant planets, was the most significant.

It was this that Dallam, having crossed the third courtyard and at last deep inside the Topkapi, now began to get ready for the final and by far the most important demonstration, that in front of Sultan Mehmed III.

The Harem

Dallam was to return to the 'Surralia' early each day and leave late each evening for a month. And if anyone ever doubted his veracity or his accuracy his account here confirms both. It is clear from his description that he set up the organ in the groin-vaulted Garden Portico, a double-columned chamber now open only along one side and attached at one end to the circumcision room and along the back to the outer façade of the privy chamber.

But only roughly. Dallam describes what is today called the circumcision room as 'one little house'. He also says that the portico chamber was open along three sides, not just one (on two sides the walls went only halfway up to the eaves), and that the Ottomans had heavy hangings that could be lowered against the weather. [157]Not until Gulru Necipoglu did her research for by far the fullest and best book about the Topkapi, were old drawings found which precisely corroborated Dallam – the circumcision room had indeed been a little house on the site of the present room, and there had indeed been hangings in the portico chamber which could be rolled up and down according to the weather. There had also been, as Dallam said, a pond full of fish. The pond was, incidentally, quite large, a 'delightful small square lake' surrounded by a broad path of intricately patterned marbles and thirty fountains set along it and spouting water into the pool with, in Ottaviano Bon's words, 'a continuous, and gentle murmur'. The pool, continually filled, drained into the surrounding gardens to fill rills and to irrigate. Here the Sultan would have himself rowed in a small boat by dwarves and buffoons who he'd have pushed in to amuse himself. Sometimes, closed off from male eyes, the concubines would come and sport in it. If they caught a fish in their nets, the Sultan would reward them. All this has now, alas, vanished.

The high, impressive, open-plan portico chamber was next door to the Sultan's private quarters and the room where he slept – or slept until Murad III left it, when it became the repository of the most important religious relics, like Mohamed's mantle. It was also closely connected to the harem proper by a short passage which could be sealed off. The whole little complex was therefore at the very heart of the Topkapi and was, as Dallam well knew, somewhere 'no Christian ever [went] in there that went awaye a Christian'. He was eventually to penetrate even deeper into the palace and the harem, into regions where very few Ottomans could go, or would even dream of going if they wished to live.

[158]Dallam was tended by what he calls two jemaglanes – variously translated and interpreted. Mayes says they were ajemoglans, which meant 'raw lad.' They were probably Greek, and it is not obvious from Dallam's account if they could speak English. They seem to have become fond of him but it gradually became clear that, whatever they felt, they had been ordered to tempt him to stay on in the Sultan's service forever.

Dallam was fed from the seventh kitchen, a simple diet of boiled or roast mutton, pilaf, yoghurt and black bread – he might sometimes have had chicken or game. In fact, Ottoman cuisine, having absorbed Middle-Eastern, Mediterranean and Asian traditions, had become, as Mansel writes, 'One of the most sophisticated in the world'.[159] Mackerel stuffed, without breaking the skin, with rice, currants, pine nuts and onion; chicken breasts beaten to a pulp and flavoured with milk, cinnamon and sugar. The rich ate black caviar; the poor red. Perhaps, in the interests of temptation, Dallam may have had red caviar. He was certainly given an abundance of fresh fruit, especially grapes. If the Topkapi grapes were anything like the grapes you can buy now in Istanbul, three times the size of those imported into British supermarkets, three times as firm and delicious, Dallam's lavish praise was amply justified.

He doesn't mention what he drank. Probably water, but it could have been wine. [160]The *Koran* almost totally forbad alcohol, but this was a Muslim tradition the least observed in Constantinople. Especially popular were the sweet wines of the Aegean, Samos and Crete. They also made their own wines. The poor drank a low alcohol fermented drink called Boza.[161] But all classes enjoyed cold drinks. [162]Evliya Çelebi describes the endless flow of snow and ice from Bithynian Olympus, insulated by being packed in felt sacks and stored in pits. Sherbert and water ices, called *dondurmá*, were in great demand during summer and sold by itinerant vendors or *dondurmajis*. Dallam may not have sampled any of this but it was certainly supplied to his next-door neighbours, the concubines of the harem.

[163]The harem was one of the most influential, at times the *most* influential, institution in Constantinople. The practice of powerful men having numbers of (usually slave) women in addition to their wife or wives was very old and very widespread. It predates Islam and was common in several ancient oriental civilisations – Persian, Babylonian and so on. It was a custom in the East for conquerors to take into their harems the wives, sisters and daughters – indeed often the entire harems of the conquered. So widespread was the practice that Darwin, in *The Voyage of the Beagle*, refers to it in South America, where it was a way of demonstrating wealth. Certainly, the rich in Constantinople demonstrated it like this. There remain a large number of petitions from wealthy men to the ulema begging to be excused the injunction in the *Koran* to wash thoroughly after each act of intercourse since the sounds of their washing infuriated their four (legal) wives.

Of course, there was an ordinary, perfectly sympathetic human reason for a harem: desire. But in Constantinople the institution evolved and became important from the middle of the fifteenth century and during the sixteenth century for a political reason. It was the same one that led to the practice of devshirme.

The Ottomans had observed the appalling results in countries which relied on a legitimate or undisputed male heir when one failed to emerge – the wars of the Spanish and Austrian succession, for instance, or the behaviour of Henry VIII. By making sure there was a superfluity of male heirs, these problems were avoided. Then, just as devshirme had made sure the Sultan's servants did not have factions or dynastic families tempted to cause trouble and rebellions, so concubines, supplied from captured Christian young women who would also owe everything to the Sultan, made sure of the same thing.

Harems had existed among the Ottoman Turks for a long time, but the institution had suddenly begun to increase in importance in Constantinople not long before Dallam arrived. This was because of Murad III.

[164]Vivid descriptions remain of this pleasant-sounding Sultan; one particularly detailed from 'Solomnne the Jewish man' is a letter to Edward Barton. Of medium stature, Murad was so fat he seemed to have no neck. He had a pink and white complexion like a delicate confection, large, pale, protruding eyes, and a long, flowing, almost golden beard. An 'aquiline' nose in a portrait looks rather fleshy (see illus. p. 00). He loved jewels and precious stones and wore a great many of 'inestimable value'. He was lively, clever and jovial and didn't like to personally shed blood. He loved literature and music and wrote poetry. He was very fond of his children and generous to his 'wives'.

For a long time, his 'wives' consisted of a single one, Satiye, who he married when she was thirteen. For twenty years he was faithful to her. However, she only bore him one son. This eventually began to worry everyone, including Safiye, and also the wife of the grand vizier and, especially, Murad's mother, Norbanu. They urged him to use his concubines to greater effect, and it seems he, almost reluctantly, agreed.

His reluctance rapidly vanished. He moved his bedroom from the privy chambers, one of which, the Garden Portico, Dallam was to occupy, and had a bedroom swiftly built for him in the middle of the harem. Here he soon established a new and quite different routine. His predecessors had been expected to sally out to war and conquer, and had done so. Murad had never found this sort of thing remotely congenial. He abandoned, almost fled, from the male world of the Second and Third courtyards. He spent every night in the harem, rose late and, after a late breakfast, faced up to the business of the day – seeing ambassadors, audiences with the grand and other viziers, the pashas, his generals. But he always returned to the harem for dinner. He much preferred the company of the concubines. It was more stimulating. It amused him. And there was another reason.

During Murad's reign, bribery and corruption began to get out of hand. 'Bribery,' writes Mansel, 'began to devour the edifice of empire.' The *bailo* noted that, as a result, 'he [Murad III] trusts no one and is wise to, for he knows that all the people who serve him can be easily bribed.'As a result, it was his women and the eunuchs who had 'the last word'. Some time towards the end of his rule, a discreet hole was made between the harem and the council hall. The latest and most secret political moves and information reached the harem before anyone else in the city except the most senior officials.

[165]As Murad's obsession with sleeping with his concubines grew, along with his enjoyment of their company, so did their number; in 1552, there were 230 in 1574, and soon after Murad died and a few years before Dallam arrived, there were 373. The harem grew to accommodate them. As well as the sumptuous apartments of Murad and his mother, who ruled the harem, there was a maze of passages, baths, courtyards – and rooms, over 300 of them. Visitors can see very little of all this at the moment, but most of the rooms were quite small. Constantinople can be very cold in winter, with icy winds and snow pouring down from Russia, and small rooms are easier to heat. Many of them had taps to run in recesses. And a few had rippling rivulets of water running in runnels at the side – partly the Islamic hunger for the sight and sound of water, but also to hide private and secret conversation – gossip with the Sultan, or gossip among the concubines themselves *about* the Sultan, about their converse with him or lack of it, about their loves, jealousies and desires.

The rooms in the harem were often beautiful – especially Murad's bedchamber – and made full use of the famous Iznik tiles, which took their name from the nearby town where they were made. They could create ceramic gardens with tiles of flowers, trees and bushes. [166]'A miracle of subtlety and softness of texture and technical proficiency to which no reproduction can do justice.' Some of the tiles had the red raised in gentle relief. Although the Ottomans certainly appreciated Iznik, it was not all that highly regarded and was simply referred to as 'pottery'. The Sultan himself ate off gold and silver, or green celador – a Chinese glaze which was supposed to detect and neutralise poison. The Iznik factory collapsed in 1617 and since then the tiles and jugs and plates have become rarer and rarer and more and more valuable. In the spring of 2010, Southebys held a sale in which one Iznik tile was expected to fetch £25–30,000; It went for £190,000. In 2013 a small Iznik bottle fetched nearly half a million at Bonham's.

[167]The lives of the concubines were by no means unpleasant. For centuries, Caucasian mothers sang a lullaby to their daughters – 'Live among diamonds and splendour as the wife of the Sultan.' 'Harem' has been variously translated as meaning 'sanctuary', 'palace' and 'sacred or inviolable place', none of which are contradictory. Nor were the concubines technically 'slaves', since they were all paid an allowance – and sometimes a great deal more than an allowance. Murad III seems to have been able to pick anyone he wanted to sleep with at any time of the day or night. Norbanu, his mother, and the wife of the grand vizier competed to find him new, beautiful, sexually attractive and intelligent young women. Each new find would pour his coffee when he visited. If she attracted him, she was *gözde* – 'in the eye'. If he then wanted to sleep with her, the chief black eunuch would be told and it would be arranged. Seeing that she might now be one to keep in with, the other girls congratulated her. They helped her bathe, perfumed her, gave her tips about what the Sultan liked and eventually led her to his bedroom. Or there was the night-time ceremony of the Golden Path, a corridor or passage running the length of the harem. As the Sultan passed between two long lines of concubines they would bow to him in pairs. If he fancied one, he would toss her his handkerchief – and she would sleep with him that night.

And sleeping with him was very well rewarded. Ottaviano Bon, the *bailo* who wrote about the harem in great detail in the early 1600s and is, as I said, our most authoritative source along with Dallam, said that after the first night, when she would be called 'Ikval' or 'favourite', he would give her all the money he had in his pocket 'be it never so much'. If she excited and satisfied 'his lustful desires' he would sleep with her again and again – rewarding her each time with jewels and money. If she conceived, she was at once given a larger income and an apartment with servants. If it was she who produced the first son, a still larger income and apartment and more servants.

Once *enceinte*, a concubine's sexual relations with the Sultan came to an end. In her apartment she was expected to devote herself to her baby. No doubt she had plenty of help, but it is perhaps here, if we had a more detailed account of how they brought up and related to their children – which we don't have – we could perhaps find the roots of that affection which prompted Murad III and Mehmed III to allow such authority to their mothers, the valides. But the territory is too speculative. These particular valides were, in any case, strong characters. And how, without any evidence or any detail, can one gauge affection? Ahmed I, who succeeded Mehmed III in 1605, had his mother executed soon after his accession.

At the end of his reign Murad III had become 'immersed in lust'. 'He had,' wrote Mansel, 'lost all restraint and was said to do justice to two or three women a night.' He lived on broth and sheep's marrow and other supposed aphrodisiacs and began to have epileptic fits. He fathered 102 children ([168]some authorities say forty-nine children – but this is not necessarily a contradiction since so many children died when young).

It was Murad III's life which caught and influenced the prurient imagination of the West. They referred, as we noted, to the whole Topkapi Palace and the court as the seraglio – a synonym for harem. The entire nation was imagined to be immersed in lust, so deeply that its imminent collapse was continually predicted since it was so 'enfeebled with continued converse with women', as George Sandys wrote in his *Relations of a Journey Begun in An. Dom. 1610.*[169] Cesare Borgia, a figure mentioned earlier, was condemned for 'living like the Turks, surrounded by a flock of prostitutes' – insulting in one sentence, as Bradford notes, both Cesare and the Turks.[170]

This prurience has considerably irritated later commentators – who depict the harem in reality as more like a very strict girls' boarding school. Or even more severe. Gulru Necipoglu says it was more like a monastery for young girls than the bordello of European imagination. She means convent, of course, a description echoed by Ottaviano Bon, who calls it a nunnery. And this was true – up to a point. The kalfalar dairesi, or headmistresses under the valides, oversaw not only much of the administration of the harem, but also the all-important education of the concubines. One of the chief aims of the harem was to create an elite class of consorts, not just for the Sultan, but as wives for the pashas and royal pages later on, when the women left the harem – as we'll see they could and did. They learnt to read and write perfect Ottoman Turkish, to read and appreciate Persian literature, to play and sing Ottoman music; they learnt various handicrafts, domestic skills, and all the nuances of Muslim religious practice. When they first arrived, they slept in dormitories. A strict silence was imposed in many parts of this convent if the Sultan was near or expected. As he walked in silent halls and corridors his shoes, studded with silver nails, sounded loudly on the marble floors to alert his women to flee at his approach.

So yes, up to a point a convent. But up to what point? On, say, the scale of chastity, not a very high one. [171]Bon rapidly makes clear he is only referring to its largely female population. As to their chastity, he explicitly contradicts it. In the dormitories, every tenth bed had an old woman to watch out for 'wantonness' – someone not really needed if wantonness never took place. In fact, Bon later writes, 'they being all young, lusty and lascivious wenches and wanting the society of men', were a prey to 'unchaste thoughts. If radishes, cucumbers, gourds or suchlike meats' were served in the nunnery, they were 'sliced, to deprive them of the means of playing the wanton.' Bon's book was based on a great many and very intensive talks with palace officials and high civil servants in the early 1600s, and there is a sense of the male imagination at work in some of his account, though quite a number of the people he spoke to would have had harems of their own. But there are other considerations.

In this nunnery, the nuns had to make love with the abbot on each visit, and with abbot Murad III these visits were frequent. Also, the concubines were tended by eunuchs, all black; [172]Some black women were also employed;

Ottaviano Bon noted "by how much the more ugly and deformed they are by so much the more are they valued and esteemed by theSultanas". By 1603, there were 111 eunuchs, which sounds a lot, but W. G. Sebald in *The Rings of Saturn* describes how by the end of the nineenth century the household of the Chinese emperor numbered over 6,000, a considerable number of whom were eunuchs.[173] In the Topkapi, by 1600, the eunuchs had often become as important as the concubines themselves. As the harem rose in influence, so did that of the eunuchs. The chief black eunuch, who controlled the discipline of the harem, could approach the Sultan, even in bed with a lover. Access led to power and power to wealth. One chief black eunuch controlled the finances of Mecca and Medina, and became so rich he built a new port at the mouth of the Danube. With no family and no descendants, the wealth of these men reverted to the Sultan on their death.

The eunuchs were captured or bought in the Sudan, and their blackness was insisted on partly for aesthetic reasons. Black provided an attractive contrast to their white turbans. We saw with the ulema that the love for boys and men was perfectly acceptable in Constantinople and the new names given to the eunuchs – Tulip, Saffron, Goldfinch, Emerald – have a distinctly flirtatious ring. This brings us to their sexuality and their potency.

The *Koran* forbids castration, so the young Sudanese were taken to Asyut on the Nile and castrated there by a Copt. [174]The operation, by which they lost their testicles but not their penis, was clumsy, crude and very painful. Many, especially the young boys, died, and it seems likely that quite a number were castrated when stronger to prevent this, when well into puberty or even as young men. In any case, very young eunuchs would not be much good at the duties of running the harem. There is also a good deal of evidence that late castration, while it may reduce it, certainly doesn't end potency. Alfred Kinsey looked at this in his *Female Report*. He was concerned with moves in America, which go on today, to castrate male sex offenders. He showed it would be useless, and his findings have relevance here. His castrates were the result of accidents or warfare. One, who lost his testicles when he was twenty-three, had a full sex life for many years. At fifty-three he was still, to use Kinsey's terms, having coitus once a week.[175] It is even possible that young men sought to become eunuchs, since it could lead to great wealth. Certainly this happened with the white eunuchs. Gazanfer Ağa, originally an Italian, who died in 1596, was sold on the slave market by pirates. After puberty, seeing where wealth lay, he had himself castrated and eventually did indeed become very wealthy.

It is possible they enjoyed whatever they gained for a long time. As far as I know there are no records of longevity among eunuchs of this period in Ottoman Turkey, but a recent *New Scientist* (29 September 2012, page 14) reported that between the mid-sixteenth century and mid-nineteenth century, Korean eunuchs lived seventeen years longer than their peers.

However often the Sultan did justice among them, the hundreds of young women can hardly have all been sexually satisfied, especially, perhaps, with Mehmed III as their Sultan. Humphery Conisby describes him, despite his sadism, as 'dull, timorous and very effeminate'.[176] After a while, usually about nine years and if they had not been 'noticed' by the Sultan, concubines were allowed to leave the harem and get married. This did not necessarily mean they were at all old – after all, Murad's wife had been thirteen when he married her, and very young girls were often chosen as potential concubines, as young as five or six.[177] Since they had been chosen for their attractiveness, their intelligence, had been well educated, and had often made not only a good deal of money but valuable contacts, they were much in demand as wives. But it is they who reveal that a good number of eunuchs were anything but impotent. [178]The historian Ali Seydi Bey wrote, 'I am witness that those black infidels are so traitorous that they may fall in love with one or two of the odalisques and spend all they earn on them. At every opportunity they meet secretly and make love ... You might ask, do the odalisques who establish relations with these eunuchs find pleasure in this? It is notorious in Constantinople that the odalisques find such pleasure. Two halberdiers of our unit, who married odalisques from the Imperial Palace, divorced them within a week when the odalisques told their husbands: "We do not enjoy relations with you as we do with the black eunuchs.'" The earlier observation by Bon that the concubines preferred the black women who served them to be ugly or deformed may be explained by them not wanting any rivals for the attentions of the eunuchs.

Apart from these liaisons, augmented by the occasional, very dangerous smuggling in of lovers, the concubines fell in love with each other. Love affairs between women were not uncommon all over Constantinople – another result, not just of human nature, but of strict segregation.

Yet there is also an air of sadness here – the sadness of someone longing for love and not being able to have it. [179]'They fell in love,' wrote Mansel, 'with men they had not seen, a voice heard singing one moonlit night on the Bosphorus; a violinist playing in the distance... the girls remained in love, knowing nothing of the beloved, for years.'

A haunting melancholy is one of the strains that characterises Ottoman music – and the concubines were taught both to play and sing and did so together frequently. It was with music in the Ottoman court that of course Dallam was most involved. And he was, together with his three colleagues, still busy setting up and making sure that the organ worked perfectly in mid-September 1599.

The Organ, Dallam and Lello

This work was finally finished on 15 September, though it was to be a further ten days before Dallam got to demonstrate it.

Incidentally, although the Ottomans hadn't the faintest idea what an organ was, Constantinople was where organs in the West had come from (though the origins of the organ were long before the city was founded). You can see today, at either end of the frieze near the base of the obelisk Theodosius erected in Constantinople at the end of the fourth century AD, an outline, somewhat weathered, of an eight-pipe organ with two boys jumping up and down to work the bellows with their feet. By the ninth century AD,

Constantinople was famous for its organs. [180]Charlamagne ordered one in 812 – legendary for the delicacy of its sound. It had 'such a soft and sweet tone that women died in transports of ecstasy on hearing it'. From this organ, all Western organs descended, some growing much coarser in a Western way – Wulston (d.963) describes an organ at Winchester, an enormous one worked by seventy men 'waving their arms and dripping with sweat ... that the full-bosomed box may speak with its 400 pipes ... like thunder the iron tones batter the ear'. There were complaints later that organs made too much noise. Nevertheless – though no one then knew this – the Levant Company's gift can be seen as a graceful compliment to the city where organs had originated.

It didn't take seventy men to work Dallam's organ. Indeed, it didn't require anyone at all. But it is very difficult to be precise about what exactly it did need. We don't have the full contract, and the partial account we have from *The Illustrated London News* of 1860 is fairly general and leaves a lot to the principal engineer, the horologist Randolf Bull. I outlined much earlier some of the complicated but indefinite specification – '... wheels and pinions ... connecting clockwork, barrels and pipes ... ' and so on. Even professional writers about organs are clearly baffled. Stephen Bicknell in his *The History of the British Organ* (CUP, 1996) talks vaguely – vague for the only time – about a barrel mechanism set off by a clock, a complicated automaton with mechanical toys.[181]

It isn't even possible to be sure what drove Dallam's organ clockwork – whether weights descending like grandfather clocks, or by wound springs or by a combination of both. [182]Boston and Longwill assume weights descending, but Randolf Bull's surviving works are watches and are spring driven, though he was certainly familiar with both. [183]There is a record of him repairing one of the king's clocks in March 1617, for instance. Spring-weight clocks were invented around 1277.

[184]But one significant element worth noting is the barrels (Dallam uses the plural). Certainly, Bull didn't invent this. A system of varied pins or protruberances on a revolving barrel (or barrels) to open and shut the

vents in the pipes, either directly or using the keys, was not new. William of Malmesbury (d.1142) records one being built for Pope Silvester, the drum being turned by a water wheel and the bellows made of buffalo skin. But as far as I can see from the six authorities I have used there is no further mention of a combined key-barrel mechanism in England until Dallam, and not after him till 1700. They didn't become popular until after 1800. Dallam's organ was therefore extremely unusual in 1599, quite apart from its intricately worked mechanical additions.

When he had to demonstrate this extraordinary instrument depended on the Sultan. The days passed and nothing happened, Lello and Dallam had to wait. Lello, who had already waited so long, grew increasingly apprehensive. Dallam seemed calm enough. He continued to go to the seraglio every day, where the ajemoghlans were now even more active 'with many perswetions' to get him to agree to stay on and serve the Sultan.

It would seem he sometimes remained at the seraglio until very late indeed. On the night of 24 September, for instance, he witnessed one of the wonders of Constantinople – the celebrations for the birth date of the Prophet. Hundreds of thousands of small lamps and candles were deployed on all the mosques, palaces, the public and private buildings and the shops. The winding streets were outlined. So were all the little ships, with red, blue or green paper lanterns swinging from their rigging, until the Golden Horn and the Bosphorus seemed to be on fire; indeed the whole mighty city blazed with religious fervour. This display took place, if not quite so spectacularly, at all important religious festivals and at royal circumcisions and weddings. Private picnics at night were also elegantly illuminated, sometimes with tortoises creeping about among the flowers with lights fixed to their shells.

Finally, the Sultan let it be known when he wished to see the presentation. The night before, Lello called Dallam into his 'chamber'. It is evident, as MacLean points out, that there was a good deal of competition about what they all got from the Ottomans. Both Dallam and Lello knew how unusually well rewarded, not just Pindar but even the humble coachman, Dallam's friend Ned Hall, had been after delivering the coach to the Sultana Safiye. The first thing Lello did, in case Dallam was expecting the same, was to warn him that, though he certainly deserved it, he should expect no such largesse himself from the Sultan – a sensible and kindly warning for which Dallam thanked him. Indeed, he presages his account of the speech, which he gives at length, with 'The Imbassadores Spetch unto me in Love after he had given me my charge'.[185]

But the bulk of the speech is really an expression of how neurotically anxious Lello still was. He was terrified the Sultan may not like the organ or that it may not work properly – in which case the Sultan would have it smashed to pieces in front of him. He was clearly – knowing Mehmed's fearsome reputation – frightened of him whatever happened. Neither he nor Dallam should on any account turn their backs to him. In fact, Dallam shouldn't expect to see the Sultan at all.

Dallam reassures him after this 'frendly spetch'. The merchants had already warned him to expect nothing extra. As for the organ, it now looked even better and was working better than when he'd shown it to the queen.

And so the two men parted, both no doubt fairly strung up. But of the two, Henry Lello was by far the most tense. The next day, everything was to be put to the test.

The Sultan Sees the Organ

Dallam left for the Topkapi soon after dawn on 25 September. He was accompanied once again by his three colleagues – his mate John Harvey the engineer, Rowland Buckett the painter, and the joiner Michael Watson.

Two hours later, Lello followed with his retinue. It is worth noting that this was not the least part of the whole enterprise. One reason the public celebrations of the Sultan's power and wealth – at births, sons' circumcisions, the marriage of a daughter, and so on – were so magnificent is that as a result of their splendour and their frequency Constantinople had developed an appetite for them. This meant that ambassadors and their retinues, their own accompanying shows of power, the lavishness of their dress, all had to impress not just the Sultan but his people as well. Philippe du Fresne Canaye, riding with the French ambassador to the Topkapi in 1573, said, 'The bank was so full of people and the walls and neighbouring houses packed to the roofs with so many spectators that I have never seen so many people at the same time in my life.'[186]

Dallam, who had watched them get ready, describes the richness of their clothes, descriptions he often gives in some detail – cloth-of-gold, thick silk capes and so on – with Lello himself 'Lyke unto a kinge, only he wanted a crown'. As they embarked from Galata, the *Hector* fired a resounding salvo from her twenty-seven guns. The retinue was fifty strong – twenty-eight on horseback (the horses probably provided by the Sultan), the rest marching. Included among the riders were the Aldridge brothers, William from his consulate on Chios, Jones from his at Patras. They, like the other merchants, knew that the success of their livelihoods depended at that moment on the success of the present and the degree they could impress the Ottomans.

Back in the Topkapi, Dallam and his men got the organ ready for its performance. The portico chamber was set on high ground looking out over the Golden Horn. Beyond, the Bosphorus sparkled in the distance. And it was racing along the Golden Horn that the servants on the look-out at last saw the Sultan speeding towards them. Like everything to do with him, this was designed to impress. [187]His kayik – narrow, elegant, forty-metres long – was rowed at such a pace by its twenty-six bostancis that, even in the nineteenth century, an identical craft could still easily outpace a boat driven at full speed by steam and propeller. Normally, the Sultan would have passed to and fro a few times, saluted by gunfire from nearby ships, but today, impatient to see at last his much-reported-on present, he made straight for the nearest shore below his palace.

This was about half a mile below the portico chamber. As soon as they saw the royal kayik coming towards them 'wythe marvalus greate speed' the ajemoghlans ran back and told Dallam and his friends they must leave the chamber at once. Dallam set the organ and they did so, the door being locked behind them.

Ear pressed against it, Dallam heard the commotion of a great crowd being let in through another door, a silence, and then the concerted 'wonderinge noyses' as they saw for the first time the organ, newly gilded and freshly painted in what the contract had described as its rich colours, standing, extraordinary for Ottomans' eyes to see, sixteen foot tall. Dead silence again as the Sultan entered and seated himself on 'his chaire of estate', then, set by Dallam to go off a quarter of an hour after he had been hurried out of sight, the organ began to perform.

And now for the first and only time we learn from the maker – or co-maker – exactly what this clock-organ could do – or rather, some of the things it could do.

'Firste the clocke strouke 22; then the chiume of 16 bels went of, and played a songe of 4 partes. That beinge done, tow personagis which stood upon to corners of the seconde storie, houldinge tow silver trumpetes in there hands, did lifte them to theire heads, and sounded a tartarra. Then the muzicke went of, and the organ played a song of 5 partes twyse over. In the tope of the orgon, being 16 foute hie, did stand a holly bushe full of blacke birds and thrushis, which at the end of the musick did singe and shake theire wynges. Divers other motions there was which the Grand Sinyor wondered at.'

What precisely these other motions were isn't clear. The figures of the queen and the angel who turned an hourglass every hour had, as I mentioned earlier, been tactfully dropped. Dallam doesn't mention the cock crowing and fluttering its wings which had been the inspiration of the whole idea and this may have been dropped as well. The positions of the planets, the sun and moon would certainly have been included, as probably a nightingale and a further two 'personagis', one striking, in the words of the contract, 'a fine, loud and sounding bell', the other 'a greater bell'.

But about the Grand Sinyor's wonderment there can be no doubt at all.

He asked the person Dallam calls the Coppagawe – probably the kapici or head gatekeeper – if the organ would ever do all this again. The Coppagawe said it would when the clock struck the next hour. The Sultan said in that case he'd wait. Sensibly, the Coppagawe went and checked with Dallam, who explained it would go only if 'a little pin', which he'd shown him, was pushed in at the same time. They all waited. The hour struck. The Coppagawe pushed the pin – and once more, with a whirring and trumpets and shaking of wings, the organ performed again. The Sultan, sitting so close to the keys that he could have touched them, asked how they moved untouched. Was there anyone there who could play on this wonderful object? Learning that Dallam could, he asked for him to be sent for at once.

Dallam, whose account of all this is much the longest and most detailed of any other event in his diary (very aware, no doubt, as MacLean observes, that this was the first and most intimate encounter between an ordinary Christian Englishman and an Ottoman emperor)[188] was now becoming extremely nervous. He asked his interpreter if it was safe for him to go with the Coppagawe into the august presence. Half-reassured, he did so. He was amazed at what he saw. He says 400 people, all richly attired – attire which he describes – were ranged there – a number which sounds exaggerated, even if, as he says, a hundred of them were dwarves. Two hundred were pages, a further hundred deaf mutes. But far more alarming to Dallam was the Sultan himself in front of the organ, a scimitar at his side. The Coppagawe led Dallam forwards, took his cloak from him and laid it on the floor and, after a few words from the Sultan, gestured to him to play. But Dallam, seeing that this would entail turning his back on the Sultan, indeed touching 'his kne with my britches, which no man in paine of deathe, myghte dow', refused. After a bit, the Sultan said something again, and now 'with a merrie countenance' the Coppagawe gently thrust Dallam forwards. Squeezing in, Dallam had to turn his back on the Sultan and did indeed brush the Sultan's knee. And this forbidden contact became even closer because, unable to see clearly what Dallam was doing, the Sultan had 'his chaire' removed and came and sat right next to him, pushing him forwards as he too squeezed in. Dallam 'thought he had bene drawing his sorde to cut of my heade'. But the Sultan simply watched intensely, Dallam 'playing suche thinges as I coulde'.

The Sultan had been due to receive Lello quite a long time before but had been held fascinated by the organ, a fascination and satisfaction which he now expressed in a practical way. He held out behind him a bag full of gold, which the Coppagawe duly handed to Dallam. It held forty-five 'chickers'.

So it was over. Dallam was allowed out of the door 'wheare I came in, being not a little joyfull of my good suckses'.

Lello's Rows – The Sultan Tries to Keep Dallam

It had been more than a success. It had been a triumph. And 'Beinge gotten oute of the Surralia' he hurried to report it to Henry Lello who, with his company, had now been waiting over two hours for his audience.

As he arrived outside the 'greate gate' where Lello and his retinue were waiting, he saw the ambassador mounting his horse to leave – but as soon as he saw Dallam he quickly came to him 'Askinge me yf the Grand Sinyor had sene the presente. I tould him yeas, and that I had sene the Grand Sinyor and that I had gould out of his pocket, whereat he seemed to be verrie glade'.

An understatement – Lello was clearly delighted. Weeks of anxiety and doubt vanished on the instant, and he told Dallam he wanted to hear every detail as soon as they got back to the embassy. But before they could return to Galata there was a typical piece of Ottoman show-off. Two Turks told Lello he must wait. They had to watch as a thousand men, 500 on foot, 500 on horseback, paraded across the huge courtyard in front of them, 'only,' Dallam noted dismissively, 'for a show.' Once passed, Lellos's retinue was led to the water's edge and allowed to embark.

As soon as they got back, Dallam had to repeat everything that had taken place. The merchants, too, were delighted – but Henry Lello suddenly went quiet. Asked why, since everything had gone so well, he said it hadn't occurred to him for a moment that Dallam might see the Sultan or be seen by him. He, Lello, had missed a vital opportunity. Had he thought this might happen he would have spent '30 or 40*li* in apparel for me'.

A typically unnecessary regret from this highly over-anxious man, but it shows the importance everyone then attached to what they wore. Today's boringness and lack of variety in, particularly, male fashion, while perhaps removing a snobbish element in how we look at each other, has made it far less interesting and far less important. In past centuries, up to, say, 1910, clothes and personal jewellery were to an extent a uniform, often designating the sort of thing you did – butchers wore one style of clothing, apprentices another, farm labourers, professional men like doctors all different again, but, far more significant, clothing revealed class, wealth and social standing. You were what you wore. And perhaps nowhere was this more noticeable and important than in sixteenth-century Constantinople. [189]Clothes of all sorts, but kaftans of velvet, satin or brocaded silk, laced with gold or silver thread, were a major industry by 1577. There were 268 looms in the city, eighty-eight of them attached to the palace. And it was not just richness of material, size counted. For example, the great onion-shaped headdresses told something. The hat, if that's not too mundane a word, of the mufti was enormous. Nor were just commercial looms at work. The women of Constantinople did huge amounts of embroidery. 'No other empire,' says Mansel, 'has put so much energy into needle and thread.' The cumulative effect of brilliant colours, silks and satins and furs, of rubies and diamonds, (Dallam, in his long account of the presentation, had time, in his terror, to notice on the Sultan's finger 'a ringe with a diamond in it halfe an inche square'), on so many pashas and officials left foreign ambassadors and princes, according to Ottoman historians, 'astonished, bewildered, stupefied and completely enraptured'.

The Ottomans must have tried to get the organ to perform its tasks themselves because at the end of September Dallam was summoned to the seraglio again to put right various things that had gone wrong. And it was now even clearer that the success of the organ had made the Sultan more determined than ever to get Dallam to remain in Constantinople and work for him, because the ajemoghlans now redoubled their efforts 'to stay with them always'. Dallam said he couldn't – he had a wife and children who expected him back. This wasn't strictly true, but he did marry soon after his return. The ajemoghlans didn't seem to regard such bonds as particularly important and said if he stayed on he could have anything he wanted, including two of the Sultan's concubines or, if he preferred, any two virgins, the most beautiful he could find anywhere in the whole country.

When he got back that evening, Dallam told Lello what had happened. Lello advised him on no account to flatly refuse. He should 'be as merrie with them' as he could and say that if he, Lello, was happy Dallam stayed, then Dallam would be happy to stay. This, said Lello, would mean they wouldn't try and keep him by force and he would be able to devise his escape when he wanted. Whether this was good advice or not it sowed in Dallam's mind the suspicion that Lello wouldn't much mind if he did have to stay on and serve the Sultan.

On 2 October Dallam briefly notes that Lello gave a banquet for the Venetian *bailo* and various important Ottomans. The laconic entry does not reveal a good deal that was going on behind it

It was a little before this that Lello had presented his letters of accreditation and became the official English ambassador. [190] He had already reported to Cecil how the Sultan had rejoiced at Elizabeth's gifts, 'especially the instrument ... whereof he made great accompt'. In fact, his audience had been a total success. Pindar, who was there, described it to the *bailo*, Capello, who passed it on to the Doge and Venetian senate. The Sultan several times interrupted Glover's speech on behalf of Lello with polite comments, something that was unusual and highly complimentary. The *bailo* put it down partly to the Sultan's pleasure in 'the great clock'. To Cecil, Lello said that the Sultan told him 'I should receive satisfaction of all I desired'.

What he desired was a great deal; as well as confirming all previous capitulations, he had asked for seventeen additional ones, and among them was to ask that the Dutch merchants should trade under the English flag as opposed to the French. This meant that the Dutch would have to pay their consulage dues to the English. To get this concession was a major coup. But a successful present and successful stage management were not necessarily enough alone. Lello was, in fact, ultimately to triumph, but in the fierce diplomatic struggles with the French there were endless setbacks, largely because the Turks were endlessly bribeable and so could not be relied on.

The concession of the Dutch consulage was so valuable that the Sultan was only likely to apportion it to the highest bidder. The Ottomans depended on presents that were essentially bribes for a considerable slice of their income. Despite the success of the organ, or despite it at that moment, de Brèves, the French ambassador, furious at English success, at once rushed round and gave the Sultan 6,000 zecchini (say, £270,000 at today's prices). The new English request was immediately thrown out.

De Brèves was furious with Lello for a more particular reason. While waiting to go into his inaugural banquet in the palace, Lello had talked at length to Khilil Pasha, the grand vizier. Henry IV of France had recently turned from Elizabeth and, through the offices of the Pope, made peace with Spain. The grand vizier asked why and later, passing it on to de Brèves, said Lello had explained that Henry IV had left the true, Protestant religion and become a papist indolator, hence the Pope's success. And this showed, once again, that no reliance could be placed on friendship with France 'but only upon his mistress [Elizabeth] who was most constant and sincere'. One might wonder why Khalil should tell the French this. To stir things up? To divide and rule? Or perhaps to warn de Brèves to tell Henry IV that the Turks disapproved of any alliance with Spain.

If to divide and also stir things up, it was immediately successful. [191]De Brèves hurried in a rage to Capello and said he was going to make an open and dramatic display of his resentment on the spot. Capello had great difficulty calming him down. He said it was probably a translator's error. Glover had made a similar mistake before in trying to describe to Ottomans the difference between papists and Lutherans, as the English were called. (That the French were idolators was an old English argument.)

Lello, unaware of the diplomatic storm he had raised up, politely asked de Brèves to his banquet. The French ambassador angrily refused. Relations were eventually restored, but all this meant Lello's official ambassadorship started under a cloud.

None of this did Dallam mention. Indeed, he probably knew little about it. Besides, he had suddenly, on 12 October, once again been summoned to the seraglio.

Dallam Sees the Concubines

The moment he arrived in the Topkapi it was immediately clear why Dallam had been sent for. The ajemoghlans had been ordered to again redouble their efforts to persuade him to stay (it is probable the Sultan wanted similar clock-organs in several of his palaces). Their attempts continued for three days. They started with a tour of the Sultan's private chambers to impress on him the money that could be in store for him. He saw and wondered at carpets and cushions laced with gems, several thrones – 'chairs of estate' in one of which he was invited to sit and 'draw that sord out of the sheathe with which the Grand Sinyor doth croune his Kinge'. He also seems to have been shown a little of the Sultan's immense treasure – 'his gould and silver'.

The climax of this wooing came on the last day. If Dallam rejected the offer of two concubines, perhaps the sight of lots of them might change his mind. Leading him through a little, marble-paved court, one of the ajemoghlans pointed ahead to a small barred grating set in a thick wall, at once signalling to Dallam to go ahead and look, something he couldn't do himself.

No one, except the ugly female servants, the eunuchs and the Sultan himself, ever got so close to the concubines as Dallam was about to. His account has become almost celebrated and been quoted in descriptions of the harem ever since.

When he looked through the grating, 'I did se thirtie of the Grand Siynor's

Concobines that weare playing with a bale in another courte. [Games like this were reported by Ottaviano Bon.] At first sighte of them I thought they had bene younge men, but when I saw the hare of their heads hange done on their backs, platted together with a tasle of smale pearle hanging in the lower end of it, and by other plaine tokens, I did know them to be women and verrie prettie ones in deede.

'Theie wore upon theire heads nothinge bute a little capp of clothe of goulde, which did but cover the crowne of her heade no bandes a boute their neckes, nor anything but faire chains of pearle and a juell hanging on their breste, and juels in their ears; their coats weare like a soldier's mandilyou [cloak], som of reed sattan and some of blew, and som of other collers, and graded like a lace of contraire collor; they wore britchis of scamatie, a fine clothe made of cotton woll, as whyte as snow and as fine as lane [lawn or muslin]; for I could observe the skin of their thies through it. These britchis cam done to their mydlege; som of them did weare fine cordovan buskins, and some had their leges naked, with a goulde ringe on the smale of her legg; on her foute a velvet pantioble [high shoe] 4 or 5 inches hie. I stood so longe leukinge as upon them that he which had showed me all this kindness began to be verrie angrie with me. He made a wrye mouthe and stamped with his foote to make me give over looking, the which I was verrie lothe to dow, for that sighte did please me wondrous well.'

Dragging himself reluctantly away, Dallam returned with the ajemoghlan to where he'd left his interpreter. When he told the Cornishman what he'd seen, he was warned very seriously that on no account should he let any Turk know about this. If he did, the ajemoghlan who had taken him would certainly be executed

In fact, it is inconceivable that the ajemoghlan would have taken Dallam there without express instructions from very high up. But it is true that if the ajemoghlan had himself looked on the concubines, his life might well have been in danger. Goodwin, the editor of Ottaviano Bon, describes how one of Murad III's concubines fell ill. The Sultan called in his Jewish doctor

Domenico Hierosolinitano to treat her. The doctor was only able to take her pulse with her arm poking out through a curtain. He was kept even further away when one of the princesses fell ill. Her arm, also poking through a curtain, was thickly bound in muslin. Since this was his only contact, his 'diagnosis,' writes Goodwin wittily, 'must have been an inspired guess.'[192]

Three days after Dallam had seen the concubines, on 17 October, the *Hector* was due to leave for England. Thankful to escape, Dallam quickly carried his chest and his bed onto the ship. He was not to get away so easily. Before the *Hector* could sail, a messenger arrived from the palace. On no account was the ship to depart until the Sultan had given his express permission. This at once put Lello into a panic. For one thing, any delay would be very expensive. The merchants were bound to the owners from whom they'd chartered the boat in the sum of £500 that, weather permitting, the *Hector* would leave on that day. For every day longer they would have to pay £20.

But to Lello far more worrying was *why* the Sultan had given this order. Had one of the crew or, worse, one of his own household, deeply offended some important personage, some pasha or vizier? He sent for the messenger and asked him if he knew why the order had been given. The messenger said he didn't know, but he'd heard that if the workman who'd set up the organ, that is Dallam, would not stay behind voluntarily then the whole ship would have to stay. The reason was the Sultan wanted the organ moved to a new place.

When Lello heard this 'he began to be somewhat merrie'. So, it was a very minor matter. He had Dallam come to him from the ship and said the *Hector* should sail and Dallam (it seems along with his three colleagues) must stay behind to do the Sultan's bidding as regards the organ.

Dallam wasn't in the least merry. He was absolutely furious. His suspicions were now fully confirmed. Lello had betrayed him. He had, Dallam raged, turned him over to the Turks. He would lead a slavish life forever, 'and never companie againe with Christians'.[193]

Lello 'verrie patiently gave me leve to speake my mynde'. Then, when

Dallam was at last calmer, he put his hand on his shoulder and said he'd no idea the ship would be stopped like this. He had no intention of allowing Dallam to be forced to stay behind. When he had moved the organ, he could go as soon as he liked. Lello would in any case have advised against going with the *Hector*. The ship was going via Scanderoon and this would both take much longer and also involve a strong risk of either malaria or plague. When Dallam did go, probably by land, he, Lello, would make certain he was compensated financially. At this, Dallam's rage and distrust vanished. 'My Lorde did speake this so frendly and nobly unto me that upon a sudden he had altered my mynde and I tould him that I would yeld my selfe into Godes hand and his.'

Soon after this dramatic exchange, Dallam and his interpreter hurried back to the seraglio, and he now learnt where he was expected to move and then reassemble the organ. It was in the Pearl Kiosk.

The Topkapi kiosks were miniature palaces, beautifully decorated and richly built, usually of wood, and set outside and about the main buildings, most on the seashore. Because there were no tides, they could be set right at the water's edge, and the sight and sound of the waters, the reflections on walls and ceilings gave, in Mansel's felicitous phrase, a feeling of floating on the Sea of Marmara or the Bosphorus. Rooms were crossed by channels of water and fountains threw water into the air and the kiosks resounded to the sweet sound of it falling back.[194]

And of all the kiosks, the Pearl Kiosk, which we briefly looked at when Murad watched the *Hector* perform for him, was the richest and the most beautiful. It was the favourite of the sultans. Dallam, some of whose account is lost on a missing page, describes it at some length. Some of his significant details like, for instance, the lead-covered pyramidical roof, later replaced, have been verified by drawings done towards the end of the seventeenth century, just as his account of the portico chamber was confirmed by later drawings. Gulru Necipoglu quotes him at length. The kiosk, placed on the sea wall looking out over the Marmara on one side and gardens on the other, had a domed hall eleven metres wide, with rooms on either side for favourite concubines, a small bathroom, a kitchen, a prayer room and lavatories. It was known as the Pearl Kiosk from the exquisite pendant globes with pearl-strung tassels hanging from the dome. The pearls were huge – brought from Baghdad, Basra and Bahrain. The nine pendant globes echoed the nine celestial spheres, the domed construction echoed the 'lofty pavilion' of the heavens. The arched portals and window frames were silver gilt, set with opals, rubies and emeralds and inlaid with porphyry, marble, jet and jasper. The carpets were Persian silk, spread with cushions of gold cloth and gold-embroidered brocade.

Alas, long vanished, the groin-vaulted basement only remaining, the kiosk had been built for Murad III between 1588 and 1591 by Grand Vizier Sinan Pasha, and it was from here that Murad, and later Mehmed, watched the salutes of visiting warships. Indeed, the kiosk could be said to have finished Murad off. One day in 1595, now having epileptic fits, subsisting entirely on aphrodisiacs, he was exhausted by his concubines, and 'clearly feeling unwell and gloomy,' writes Gulru Necipoglu, 'he asked his musicians to sing him a song. The lyrics ran "I am sick, come Destiny and take my life tonight."' As the musicians sang their doleful melody, some ships from Alexandria fired their guns in salute, as custom demanded. But the ships were too close, the explosions too powerful. They shattered ten jewel-surrounded windows and the whole kiosk shook violently. The Sultan, already ill, took this as an omen. He died several hours later.

The organ's removal seems to have had nothing to do, at that point, with the Islamic relics stored next to the portico chamber, as has been suggested – after all, there was a religious prayer room with relics in the kiosk – but because, as Dallam realised, the Sultan wanted to show it off to his concubines and this was much more easily and comfortably done in the kiosk.

Dallam was laying out the pipes, barrels and other constituents of the organ on the jewelled carpets when he noticed that the ajemoghlans who had been with him had all vanished. Asking why, his interpreter told him that it was because the Sultan was approaching with some of his concubines and that they too should flee at once – whereupon, clearly terrified, he shot off, leaving Dallam behind.

Now, frightened himself, Dallam ran after him and was at once pursued by '4 blackamoors ... with their several semetaries drawn'. He raced towards the nearest gate and reached it just in time to slip through. He found a crowd of anxious ajemoghlans 'praying that I myghte escape the hordes of those runninge wolves'. He did not pause, but at once took a boat back to Galata. Dallam was right to be afraid. One might think that because he was a Frank in the service of an ambassador and under the jurisdiction of the Levant Company he would have been safe, but this is not so. Probably the Sultan, had he seen what was happening and had he recognised Dallam, might have intervened to save him, but his over-zealous servants would have had no hesitation in 'hew[ing] me all in peecis with there semeteries'. [195]About sixty years later the grand vizier failed to rise when the French ambassador came for an audience. The ambassador demanded loudly that the Ottoman show him more respect. The vizier is supposed to have answered in a rage: 'Do I not know that you are an ... Infidel, that you are a hogge, a dogge, a turd eater.' During the row that followed, the Frenchman was assaulted, imprisoned and only just escaped with his life. A Dutch official who gave a 'rash answer' to a grand vizier received 184 blows to his bare feet and it was feared he would be 'crippled all his life'.

Certainly Lello, when Dallam told him about this incident, took it very seriously indeed. He hauled the interpreter in and said he would hang him for abandoning his charge in this way; in the end he banned him from the embassy.

Dallam had been told by the ajemoghlans that the Sultan would come to the kiosk the next day, 21 October, because he wanted to watch how the organ was put together again. But the 21st was a Sunday and Lello forbad anyone to work then. When Dallam got there on the Monday, he was told that the Sultan had come and was irritated not to find Dallam waiting for him. He assumed he had stayed away on purpose and said that in that case he wouldn't come to watch the reassembling of the organ again.

Few people could have had a strong enough character to resist the effects of absolute power, the incessant sycophancy and adulation, and Mehmed III was not a strong character. As well as the capricious cruelty he had often shown, he was described, noted earlier from Humphery Conisby, as effeminate and weak, but this petulant reaction to Dallam's absence – the real reason for which he would have known or been told – may have done the young man a service. The Sultan seemed to lose all interest in detaining him in Constantinople and from then on his efforts to do this stopped.

By 24 October, the organ was ready again. On the 25th, Dallam returned to the seraglio for the last time to go over it with the Coppagawe and to make sure his own work was perfect.

His task in the Topkapi was now done. He had time on his hands. He decided that, at long last, he could explore the city.

Exploring Constantinople

Dallam refers briefly to the row still simmering between Lello and de Brèves (approaching a climax) and then sets out, in a new pair of leather shoes, for the first time into the great city – and the reader has a strong feeling of his excitement.

It was 12 November, and he started at the Constantinople gate farthest from Galata, watching from there a caravan of the 'tallest camels that ever I had sene in all my time'. Then he turned back and plunged into the city itself.

I say 'he', but Dallam writes 'we' – so presumably he went with his three companions, Hall, Watson and Beckett. No doubt they felt safer in a group, but in fact Constantinople was a much more law-abiding city than, say, London or Paris at that time.[196] The streets were patrolled by Janissaries, but it was acute awareness of the huge number of summary executions flowing from the palace which paralysed would-be wrong-doers. You will remember the baker baked alive in his own oven. M. de Thévenot's *Travels in the Levant* describes how in the 1650s (but, as usual, identical in this respect to 1600) Sultan Mehmed IV enjoyed following his men, all of them incognito, into various shops and how 'one day a butcher offered to sell him meat above the rate which he had set, he made a sign to the executioner who ... cut off the butcher's head'.

Nor was the populous overtly unfriendly. This was less so in the provinces, and early in the sixteenth century visitors to Constantinople had to wear Ottoman dress and grow beards, but by the time Dallam and his friends were there this was unnecessary and they could be in their Western clothes. They were also able to dispense with the services of one of the six or seven Janissaries attached to each embassy to accompany anyone who went out. Sometimes a stone or an apple core might be thrown by children, but the same thing happened in London to well-dressed men and women and foreigners. That Dallam could wear right through a new pair of leather shoes exploring and not once mention interference shows how safe the streets of Constantinople had become. The prevailing sense was of order. Order was everywhere, and not just in law enforcement. Every trade was organised into guilds (even thieves and prostitutes had their own guilds). Constantinople was far more *civilised* than Europe in many ways – the guilds provided social security and were a source of loans to members. And the palace had an official overseeing the major guilds (one assumes not the thieves and prostitutes).

[197]Safer, and also a little cleaner than London or Paris because the wide, deep and fast-flowing Bosphorus dealt more effectively with sewage than either the Thames or the Seine. The city walls were so long that most people could still live inside them in small two to four roomed wooden houses, often daubed in pastel colours, pale blue, pink, yellow. The upper storeys sometimes projected so far out you could shake hands with your neighbours opposite. The windows were heavily latticed to prevent passing men catching a glimpse of any women inside. The streets were crooked and very narrow (partly, as in Aleppo and across the whole Middle East, to provide

shade), most of them far too narrow for wheeled vehicles, which in any case did not become common for several hundred years – in 1881, for instance, they were not even known about in Morocco. Crooked, narrow, totally unplanned, a chaotic higgledy-piggledy which, because Constantinople and Galata were built on hills, were often precipitous.

[198]Mansel quotes Edmundo de Amicis, the Italian travel writer describing it in 1824, when it hadn't really changed much. 'The streets bend into infinite angles, wind about among small hills, are raised on terraces, skirt ravines, pass under aquaducts, break into alleys, run down steps, through bushes, rocks, ruins, sand, hills. Here and there the great city takes as it were breathing time in the country, and then begins again, thicker, livelier, more highly coloured ... '

None of this really exists now, any more than sixteenth-century London still exists, but you can perhaps get a feeling of that disorderly city today from the winding streets and wooden houses between Sultanahmet and the sea.

Dirty, disordered, but also beautiful. Despite that brief, blurred glimpse of wooden houses and winding streets, 'it is impossible,' writes Alexander Pallis, 'to form an idea of the splendour and fairy-like charm of the former capital of the Ottoman Empire in the heyday of its glory – that is during the 16th and 17th centuries.'[199] The juncture of glittering water and, in the palaces and mosques, rich architecture was so striking that Mansel quotes poets comparing the Bosphorus to a diamond between emeralds. Emeralds because of the verdant green of the gardens, parks, flowers and trees. This was the central feature compared to other cities of water like Venice or Amsterdam. Constantinople was full of gardens – terraced, kitchen, sunken. Towering umbrella pines clothed the heights and trees grew in the streets where there was any room and vines and wisteria and creepers climbed the walls of houses even in slum districts, and were flung across the streets like washing lines in Naples. The Sultan had sixty-one gardens along the Sea of Marmara and the Bosphorus, part of a succession of parks and orchards; people even used the graveyards for picnics since they too were invaded by greenery and colour, with weeping willows, cypresses and the flowers that were everywhere, pink, white, red, yellow jasmine, irises, roses, poinsettias, bougainvilleas, lilies, hyacinths, but above all, tulips.

[200]The Ottomans loved tulips. In 1574 Sellim II told his officials in Aleppo, 'I need 50,000 tulips for my royal gardens. I command you in no way delay.' Three years later, Murad ordered 300,000 tulips from the Crimea. This beautiful flower became the centre of intense study and debate. A perfect tulip was described, in one of Mansel's apt quotations, as 'almond-shaped, needle-like, ornamented with pleasant rays, her inner petals like a well, as they should be, the outer petals a little open, this too, as they should be'.

In the sixteenth and seventeenth centuries, tulips spread from Constantinople to Central and Western Europe, and so at last to Holland – with effects we all know. It is not surprising that the flowers were frequent gifts, form the principal motifs in embroidery and on Iznik tiles and other pottery and are celebrated in poetry.

Dallam, in this section of his diary, is plainly pushed – 'I have not time now to wryte.' He hopes for a period 'of better leasur'. [201]But he and his companions would have noticed, they may have stopped at, the endless cafés and eating houses in that gourmet capital of the world which so stimulated Çelebi's powers of description. Coffee had been introduced in 1555 from Syria. [202]Braudel describes the colossal consumption fuelling these restaurants and cafés as well as the 700,000 population. Constantinople was one of the first of what he calls monster parasite cities devouring their surroundings. As early as 1577, the slaughter of mutton and lamb for local consumption was forbidden. It was reserved for the capital. Provincials would have to make do with goat or beef. Braudel quotes some astonishing figures. One of his sources (among others) Robert Mantran gives an idea of the great city's appetite in the middle of the seventeenth century, but it would have been much the same when Dallam was there. One hundred and thirty-three bakers needing 500 tons of grain a day, 200,000 cattle eaten every year ('one has,' Braudel agrees, 'to read the figures two or three times before one can believe them'), almost four million sheep, three million lambs, barrels of honey, sugar, rice, skins and sacks of cheese, caviar, and almost 7,000 tons of butter which came by sea. 'These figures,' Braudel ends, '[are] too precise to be accurate, too official to be entirely false. They came from Turkish documents in the Bibliotheque Nationale in Paris and give some idea of the order of the operation.'

Dallam and his companions felt, and were, relatively safe as they explored this ordered city. But in the longer term this safety and security rested on thin ice. [203]Terrible fires could sweep through the wooden houses – one was believed to have been started by sailors and soldiers in 1555 so that they could loot and rape in the ensuing panic. There was another destroying 7,500 wooden shops in 1564, another in 1729 – and others. Also, Constantinople, (and of course now Istanbul), was built on a tectonic fault line, subject to devastating earthquakes – it was shattered in 1509, again in 1645, again in 1719, 1766 and 1894. More will inevitably come. Earlier, wooden houses were marginally safer. Today it is all concrete, cement, stone, brick and steel.

Returning to Galata each night, pressed for time afterwards, there is, of course, a good deal Dallam doesn't comment on. He doesn't talk, for instance, about the sounds of the city, about the gulls, which then, as now, because of the sea all round Constantinople, were bigger and noisier and more numerous than the gulls of London he was used to.

He doesn't mention the calling of the faithful to prayer from the minarets of the mosques. Ringing out five times a day, even now the sound can for a moment rise above the traffic. There is something soothing about its regularity. 'God is great. I testify there is no god but Allah. I testify that Muhammed is the prophet of Allah. Come to prayer! Come to salvation! God is great. I testify there is no god but Allah.' And in 1600 there were over 300 mosques in Constantinople. There were, of course, no cars, and unlike London at the time almost no horses or carriages. There was, compared to today, silence. [204]Even in 1810, a British traveller, Dr Meryon, said that the streets were 'so silent that people's voices were heard as if in the next room.'

And at night, when Dallam had returned to the embassy, they were quieter still. [205]Orhan Pamuk describes the distant barking, sometimes howling of dogs, the faint sounds from the wooden houses, in winter the faint glimmer of the light from their windows reflected off the snow.

But when Dallam returned to the embassy for the last time, the leather soles of his new shoes worn right through, he collapsed. For ten days he lay, he wrote, 'With a burning fever and in great dainger of my life.' When he got up, he could hardly walk.

Nevertheless, at the end of November, there came a chance for him to escape Constantinople forever. Weak as he was, Dallam grabbed it.

Escape

So bad and so difficult were relations becoming with the French that Henry Lello had decided to send Paul Pindar with a small party back to England to explain things to Robert Cecil. It was this party Dallam asked to join.

At the end of October, Lello had written to Cecil explaining that French bribes had persuaded the Sultan to withdraw all concessions Lello had recently been granted. His angry complaints were simply referred back to the grand vizier, Khalil Pasha. As a result, Lello had let the *Hector* slip away with none of the customary explosions of cannon and other ceremonies. This seems to have made the Ottomans sit up. The queen mother, Lello's main ally, was devastated. She had prepared a valuable present for her great friend Queen Elizabeth in return for the coach – a present including a tiara set with rubies (typically rubbished by Sanderson). More importantly, or just as important, England was still at war with Spain. This was supposed to keep Spain from attacking Turkey. England was vital. The Sultan, strongly urged on by the valide, quickly agreed that all capitulations would be restored, including the Dutch coming under the English flag. But could Lello believe this would last?

It was all this he needed Pindar to tell Cecil. It was also necessary to have the valide's present transported to England.

As for Dallam, Lello didn't want him to go. Not because of anything to do with the organ or the Sultan, but precisely 'because I was verrie wayke'. The journey was bound to be extremely arduous and he was anxious on Dallam's behalf. Dallam begged to be set free to join the group who, he says, 'weare all desierus to have my company'. This is probably true. Dallam was a good companion and had become very popular. He would also be a useful man to have along.

In his diary, Dallam also says he wouldn't have had another chance like this for two or three years. This isn't strictly true. Levant Company ships came more frequently than that. You will remember that between 1583 and 1588, company ships made twenty-two voyages to the Levant – and that was right at the start of this continually expanding trade, so it is unlikely he pushed this argument with Lello. Nevertheless, the ambassador was eventually persuaded. He then behaved with the consideration that, in fact, he had always shown. They were to start the journey by boat and carry on the bulk of it over Greece by land. Lello ordered Dallam's bed to be carried out onto the ship, and gave instructions that, once they had landed, he was to have a horse to ride and a second horse to carry all his things.

And so, on Wednesday 28 November, 1599, at four o'clock in the afternoon, he and the rest of them set off for England.

CHAPTER 6

The Return

Setting Out

Paul Pindar's little band embarked for England on what Dallam calls a 'carmesale', a two-masted, square-sailed brig, for what he describes as a 'discontented voyage' due to the captain and crew being so 'barbarus'.

The party consisted of Dallam himself and, though he doesn't mention them except for John Harvey once, his whole team together with Paul Pindar, Humphery Conisby, a merchant, William Hickockeys and an interpreter – eight in all. The interpreter would have interested and pleased Dallam. His name was Finch and he had been born at Chorley in Lancashire, not far from where Dallam himself had been born. He was to prove resourceful and loyal.

The strong current and a following wind carried them swiftly down the Dardanelles. Passing 'Troy' again the next day, and then bearing out south-west, they reached the island of Lemnos on 1 December. Here the wind became so strong that they had to wait at anchor. There must have been some sort of altercation with the barbarous captain and crew because Dallam says they were 'in greate dainger of beinge caste awaye'.

There was the usual toing and froing of contrary winds before they could sail off again, but by 9 December they had crossed the 130-odd miles south-west across the northern Aegean and landed at Volos at the northern top of the Pagasaen Gulf (Gulf of Pagasai). The following day they hired horses and mules. For eight men they had twelve animals, the mules being kept for their kit, including the Sultana's valuable present for Queen Elizabeth. They also carried enough food and water for three or four days. Frequently sleeping rough, it was, as Dallam points out, often impossible to buy 'vitels' at the few little villages. There was a great deal to carry, including, as Lello had ordered, Dallam's bedding – but mules are astonishingly strong. [206]Darwin, in *The Voyage of the Beagle*, describes how on level ground they could carry loads of 416 lbs (29 stone); in mountainous country, which Pindar's party was soon to reach, 100 lbs less.

On 10 December, they set off into Greece, and following them we at once run into problems. These seven pages of Dallam's diary are from one point of view the most interesting of the lot. Sailors, merchants and curious travellers had been coming to the Middle East and the Levant for a great many years. It was certainly extraordinary that an Elizabethan craftsman in Dallam's position should make such a journey and even more extraordinary that he should keep a diary; but there are quite a number of other descriptions with which to augment what he wrote. However, as far as I can see, no one else until Dallam left any sort of account of the wild, bleak mainland over which he now travelled. His diary here is unique, but it can't be corroborated or added to.

It is also often difficult to see what route he and the rest of Paul Pindar's party followed. Dallam was to show he was still as ready as ever to explore and see new places, but he was in a hurry to get home. There are gaps in the diary. In his haste, he makes mistakes. At one point, for instance, he writes 1699, meaning 1599, when he should have written 1600. And, apart from anything, the journey was extremely tough, by far the hardest part of his whole expedition. Keeping a diary must have been very difficult.

Nevertheless, we can follow them all approximately. At first they rode due south following rough tracks parallel to the coast of the Pagasaen Gulf, and then west along the Gulf of Lamia reaching Lamia itself by nightfall on 12 December – three days. By motorway, roughly duplicating the route, it is 123 kilometres.